THE
SPIRIT
HAS SPOKEN

One Man's Disobedience Caused a Mystery, Only
the Voice of God Could Solve

Eva Bellamy

Published By: Tel A Vision Publishing, LLC

Re-released Copyright © 2022

Secretarial State TXu 1-096-855

Original Copyright © 2004 by Eva Bellamy

Official Published 2008

ISBN: 978-0-9794065-3-9

Cover Designed: Angela Brand Enterprise

Typography: Tel A Vision Publishing, LLC

Copyediting: Tel A Vision Publishing, LLC

Printed in the U.S.A.

Special Thanks

I give God the thanks for life, and the birthing of this book. Special thanks for my branding & life coach and sister for life Angela Brand. You've always supported my dreams and vision. And I am grateful for all the others who have been in my corner through this journey. Thank you all, Peace and Blessings....

Contents

Acknowledgements

A special acknowledgement goes to my mother, Dorothy Bellamy as she rests in peace. I know if she were still alive here on this earth, she would be so proud of me.

To my father, Hosea Fairley, thank you for all your wisdom and counsel that you have given me over the years. I love you much.

Special thanks to my children, Kendra and Kamrin. You both are my delight and inspiration. Mom knows that it hasn't been easy for us, but you all have encouraged me over the years to keep believing and dreaming, all because of you. I love you both so much.

To all the prayer warriors who spent countless hours interceding for me and the vision God placed within me. Thank you for standing in the gap on my behalf and loving me through your prayers.

Sincere thanks to everyone who opened up their home to me and gave me shelter while I went through my process of birthing out my purpose. I pray God's blessings above and beyond all you could ask or think.

Readers Response To

THE
SPIRIT
HAS SPOKEN

The lasting effect of Evie's experience on me, is the fact that I am now always careful to ask God to give me keen hearing to decipher His voice from any others, over and above all the noise that surrounds me, and to follow His lead, so that, contrary to Evie, I will never acquire the tendency to succumb to the devil's voice or guidance. I pray with the hymnist, John Ernest Bode "Oh, speak, and make me listen, thou guardian of my soul."

Rosalind Arthur-Andoh, Ph. D

"The Spirit Has Spoken" displays how God orders your steps to deliver you out of your sins. Your deliverance comes in your ability to obey His voice.

Pamela Theresa White, Ph. D

The book written by Eva is a very spiritual, but interesting novel on how we must listen to our most inner being – Our spirit man. I can't wait to see this book hit stores. It will be a blessing to many readers.

Bishop Derrick Ford

This book is so what is needed now in a World that relies on videos and TV to lead their vision on their right to judge others. "The Spirit Has Spoken" allows the reader to be aware of the destructive path a person can or may take when they have not allowed God to lead their steps; and have faith even in the mist of circumstances that may not be in their control. You are not only reading a tremendous book but are granted the benefit of an unforced Bible Study in the process. Thank you for being inspired and obedient to the call, to write this book.

LeKeisha Dudley

"The Spirit Has Spoken" was written very well and it does a great job explaining how good and evil is always present. Spirits will speak to anyone regardless of age, race or gender. Lastly, it made me realize the importance of knowing the voice of God.

Marita R. Palmer Cosby

Phenomenal! "The Spirit Has Spoken" was an excellent, inspirational book.

Priscilla Mangum

Introduction

The mid 80s were the good old days for Evie Young. Sunday mornings were about going to church with her mother, Ada, and father, Jerald. After service, they would go to the all-you-can-eat buffet, where all church people went. Those were the memories Evie had to store deep down in her heart. After her parents' disappearance when she was eight, she experienced devastating moments in her life. With Evie's parents missing, her life became a mystery that only the voice of God could solve.

If you are reading this, that means you are still alive. And at some point, in your life, you have said to yourself "Man I should've just listened to my gut feeling, and why didn't I follow my first damn mind?"

From my experience and just like you can attest, you have learned and still is learning that your intuition will never lie, never fail you, and never steer you wrong. As we go through life, for some reason or another, we fail to listen to that small still voice within because, we want what we want. After all we are free- willed beings and we have the power to make our own choices we just have to face the consequences that it comes with, whether they good or bad.

This book was written with the intentions to assist readers to further understand the importance of listening to that inner guidance that helps us to make better choices. In the pages of this book, we will explore how Evie learned the different between the good voice, the bad voice, her free-will and how it has impacted her life.

Now let's hear what **"The Spirit Has Spoken."**

Chapter One
Death Dreams

In the heart of Atlanta, Georgia, Evie Young lied in her luxury hotel suite. The rain beats against the tall, tinted window of the bone, stucco building. Thunder and lightning strike through the opening of the draped window. Raindrop dripped, cast a shadow on the wall; Tracey nudged Tank to wake up.

"Yo Tank!" Tracey whispered, while shaking him, stretched out next to Evie. She is wrapped in a beige-colored sheet; her left leg hung from under it.

"Tank man, get up!" Tracey insisted, shaking him. "Get up!" Tracey prodded, until Tank finally opened his eyes.

"What man?" Tank looked up as his broad shoulders and masculine chest arise. Looking around, he sat up like a dead man in his black boxers.

Tank daydreamed while looking at the deep, wine-colored carpet. He turned around and looked at Evie's right French manicured hand, stretched out over a pillow. Tracey laid Evie's rolling suitcase on the floor and unzipped it. He began rambling through her stuff while picking up her black garter belt from the floor. He dug out several G-strings along with other exotic outfits. Tracey pulled out Evie's black thigh-high patent leather boots. Angry and frustrated, he dumped the rest of her suitcase onto the carpet, and everything tumbled out.

"Trick, where's my money?" Anger displayed on his forehead. Tank stood up in his dark denim jeans, walked toward the foot of

1

the bed and picked up his cream-colored shirt. Tracey discovered exactly what he was looking for. Large bills of cash held in his hand, with an enlarged smile on Tracey's face. He then folded it and puts the money into his khaki pants. Evie moaned while turning her head and tossing it back. Tracey and Tank looked at each other. Tracey then looked at the needle on the round table near the bathroom. He walked over and grabbed it and then took out two, four-ounce bottles of liquid Heroin.

"Tracey, what are you doing?" Tank snapped at Tracey, watching him tap the tip of the filled needle. "We've already drugged her enough."

"I want this bitch dead. Had you been on your game when I told you to keep an eye on her at the club, we wouldn't be having this conversation. So...step pretty boy!" Tracey sarcastically smiled at Tank.

Evie laid on her stomach tossing her curly black hair back and forth on the pillow while trying to awake. Tracey walked over to Evie. She continued to moan.

"Yeah, moan trick moan. Big Daddy has a treat for you!" Tracey seduced Evie, kissing her neck. Tank walked to the foot of the bed, with an angry eye, pressing his teeth together. Its force reflected on his structured jaw. Tracey pulled back the covers as the muscles in Evie's back reflected through her shiny, honey-brown skin. He began to kiss her from the dip in her lower back working his way up.

Tracey's body relaxed on hers while he kissed her neck from behind, her ear through her curly black hair. Tracey reached in his left pocket, takes out a tourniquet, and tied it tightly around her left arm. He then took the needle and injects it. Evie slightly jumped while letting out a loud moan. "You like that?" Tracey whispered in her ear.

Tank looked angry at Tracey, walking towards exit. Evie stopped moaning. Tracey released the tourniquet from her arm and placed it back into his left pocket.

"That's enough Tracey. Let's go!" Tank urged. Tracey turned around, looking over his shoulder at Tank, while the needle continues to drain into Evie's veins. He took out the needle and placed it on the floor beside the bed. He stood up while Tank opened the front door, released the handle, of the door. Tracey pulled the shuts. Tracey covered Evie with comforter, leaving her arm hanging over the side of the bed. He looked down on her, smudged his hand through her hair.

"Give a trick a treat and she die to sleep," Tracey smirked. Grabbing his car keys, he walked toward the exit and hits the light switch; Evie stiffly laid.

"Yo' Tank, what was that all about?" Tracey questioned Tank as both men walked down the carpeted hallway toward the elevator.

"I'm straight!"

"Nigga, you ain't straight! You liked that ho!" Tracey stared at Tank. The two men approached the elevator; stood face-to-face towards each other.

"Evie was different from the rest of the chicks in the club. You had no reason to OD her. Your intentions were to kill her." Furiously, Tank balled his fist at Tracey.

"Your soft ass, I should've killed! And different! Pssh... The only difference I see is, the ho left the club without paying me my money, and her pelvis gripped yo dick so hard, it clogged your mind! Rule number one, in this game bruh, you don't catch

feelings for a stripper. Period! I don't care how good it is! So put your heart back in its place before I do!" Tracey reached for his G47. Aiming it at Tank's chest. "You trippin?" Tank eyed Tracey's gun aimed at him, he swallowed hard. "Yeah!"

With a hard stare, Tracey placed gun back on his hip. "Good . . . partner?" Tracey playfully punched Tank in the arm. The elevator rang and the doors opened. Three sexy females stood before them. Tracey tapped Tank's right hand.

"Money time!" He licked his lips and walked inside the elevator with a smooth gait. Tank followed closely behind. The elevator door closed as Tracey walked up to the tallest girl and began his flirtatious gestures, playing his usual game – pimpin.

◆ ◆ ◆ ◆ ◆

The clock in room 666 displays 4:40 a.m. In the hotel room, Evie's body laid across the bed lifeless. The storm had past, and the rain had stopped beating on the tall, tinted windows. The aroma of drugs and sex hovers in the dark, cold room, being left for dead.

◆ ◆ ◆ ◆ ◆

Ten years before...
Evie sat on mom's lap that's covered with a silk purple nightgown. She rocked in an ancient-wooden rocking chair, while expressing her love.

"Momma."

"Yes, baby," Ada responded gently.

"I love you so much," Evie looked up at her mother and smiled.

"And I love you more!" Ada rubbed Evie's silky hair.

"Mommy," Ada answered with a hum and smiled. She continued to rub her hair while sliding her manicured toes out of her bedroom slippers.

"Ms. Gram, my Sunday school teacher, taught us today how God sent mommies to guard over His little children until we go back home to be with Him forever."

"And that is true."

"Do you know what else I learned besides Jesus dying for me mommy?"

"And what is that baby?" Ada inquired with a smile.

"Mothers are special and that's why I love you so much. God could've picked someone who was mean and ugly, but He chose you because you're beautiful and sweet like, the chocolate chip cookies you bake for me every day." Ada stopped rocking and gently turned Evie around, so they are face-to-face. Tears formed in Ada's eyes as she responded.

"Aww Evie, thank you honey! That is the sweetest thing I've ever heard."

Meanwhile Jerald approached the doorway of Evie's bedroom and propped his hand on the top of the doorpost. He looked at his wife and daughter. Ada continued to bond with Evie. A teardrop rolled down her high cheeks.

"I would never trade you for nothing in the world!" Ada gently shook her head back and forth. "If something should ever happen to you or your father before God took me home to be with Him, I would be lost!" Jerald smiled at the words from Ada's lips. She began to sing to Evie.

"You are a part of me, a blessing sent from above, and I am so thankful for all your love; there's no one who compared to you and you are safe in my arms, just where you belong!" Ada finished the song with humming. She closed her eyes, holding Evie close while gently resting her chin on top of Evie's head.

Jerald softly walked into the room to wrap his large masculine arms around his wife and daughter. He placed one side of his cheek on Ada's face. She opened her eyes slowly, slightly cracking an intimate smile, and kissed Jerald on his cheek. Evie looked up at her dad. Then she jumped out of her mom's lap.

"Daddy!"

"How's my princess?" Jerald kissed her forehead.

"I missed you all day. Daddy!"

Ada looked up with a smile, and then stood by her husband. "How was your day. Honey?"

"Now that I've seen the two most beautiful women in my life, my day has just gotten better," Jerald kissed Ada on her lips, then Evie on her nose.

"Daddy."

Ada walked over to Evie's bed and pulled back her pink and purple comforter and tucked her in.

"Yes baby." Jerald responded.

"When are you going to pick up Justin? I can't wait!"

"Your brother will be here in the morning, and when I return you can help me unload his things off the truck."

"Yesss!" Evie celebrated.

"God answers prayer!" Ada stood next to Jerald, hugging his waist.

"You prayed that your brother would live with us and look at what God!" Ada rejoiced.

"Thank you, God!" shouted Evie.

"Well, let Daddy go so I can make it back in the morning."

"Okay Daddy!"

"Goodnight baby," Ada kissed Evie's forehead, and Jerald kissed her on the nose. Closing the bedroom door gently; they both walked down the stairs to the kitchen. Ada targeted the sliced cheesecake in the fridge. Jerald walked into the restroom.

"Honey, I have your favorite banana pudding cheesecake, with your name on it right here!" Ada dipped her finger into the

cheesecake and licked her finger, as Jerald exited the bathroom. Jerald walked over towards Ada, thrilled, she dipped her finger into the dessert and crested it into her husband's lips. Licking his lips, he rolled his eyes to the back of his head.

"Baby, that is delicious! Sweet as you." Looking at his smart watch.

"I have to get going. I told Keisha I'd meet her at the truck stop in Delaware by 2 a.m. I wanted to come home first to my beautiful wife and princess before I went." Jerald kissed Ada on her forehead while she pushed cake inside her mouth. While Ada and Jerald talked in the kitchen, Evie sneaked downstairs with an ideal question.

"We can call a babysitter to come and watch Evie so I can ride with you? You've been in that truck all day. I know you're tired. I can be right beside my husband, keeping him awake." Ada smiled, kissing him on the cheek. Evie tiptoed behind the couch eavesdropping.

"I'll be fine babe." Jerald grabbed a bottle of water out of refrigerator. Besides, it's too late to call a babysitter. We have this same conversation Ada every time I have to pick up Justin." Ada gazed at Jerald in offense, walking away from him. With an attitude, she shoved the remains of her cake into the garbage disposal. Forcefully throwing the plate and fork into the sink, Jerald walked behind her.

"Are you upset?" Ada stubbornly ignored his question.

"Is this about Keisha?" Jerald took her hand and looked into her eyes. Ada sighed, pulling away from him without answering. "I

8

see!" This is not about 'you going' and keeping me awake. This is about Keisha, isn't it?"

"We've been married for ten years Jerald, and not once have I met your ex-wife. Justin is like my son too. I love and care for him as much as you do! When he was in need, I pitched in with you to make sure he had food and clothes. During trial, we fasted and prayed together, God answered us honey. It broke my heart to find out how Keisha was abusing him." Ada deeply thought.

"But it's the fact that I never met her Jerald, out of all the years we've been married. It makes me wonder!" Ada walked away from him, taking a seat on the couch. Ada began to whisper a prayer. Jerald huffed and held his hands high. "Lord why do I go through this with this woman?" He questioned God.

"Be swift to hear and slow to speak [James 1:19]. It is Me, Jerald, the Lord your God speaking through your wife. Listen and hearken to My voice through her. For, you are to take her with you." The Spirit of God spoke.

Another voice spoke, *"She doesn't trust you. That's all! Just go by yourself!"* Jerald ignored the first voice, instead he listened to his second intuition.

"Why are you allowing worry to lead your thoughts. Ada?"

"Worry?!" Ada picked up the TV remote. Jerald took it out of her hand.

"Ada, I know you! It's written all over your face. The same expression you had for the past years when it comes to Keisha. Look at me Ada! There is no reason to feel jealous! You're the bone of my bone and flesh of my flesh!"

"Now you're accusing me of being jealous!" Ada interrupted! Jerald placed his pointer finger across her lips, quieting Ada with a passionate kiss. Evie peeked from behind the couch, and almost knocked tall gold lamp over. Jerald caressed his wife. He leaned forward as her back arched back towards the lamp. Carefully, Evie moved closer to observe the scene of her parents.

Ada sat up in anger. "Jerald, your caressing exit is old! Why haven't I met Keisha since you claim I am bone of your bone and flesh of your flesh? Why do you continue to ignore the issue?"

"Ada, it is not that big of a deal and my kiss is not an exit!" In frustration, Jerald threw his hands up. "Woman, what do you want me to do? Huh?! Say, 'sure honey, you can go' and leave our daughter with a babysitter just because you don't trust me?"

"Jerald this is not about trust! I really feel that I need to go this time! My gut has a bad feeling about you being on the road, alone this late. I can keep you awake with conversation."

"I haven't seen my wife all day and we start off on this note? It's too bad I have to leave right now because if I didn't . . . believe me, it would only take me about thirty minutes in the bedroom with you, and your whole attitude would change." Jerald changed the subject. Ada smiled.

"Yeah, I thought your expression would change." Jerald smiled.

"I miss you babe. Every moment I get, I just want to spend with you. Since your truck route doubled, you are always on the road and I just . . ." Ada paused, pulling him closer.

"Pray that God allow you to spend more time with your family, instead of being gone for months on the road. I just want us close

again Jerald! The only time we share closeness is when we are between the sheets. Then, you're gone for months, depriving my hormones. Ada smiled with a laugh.

"I won't argue with that one! But... I'll change! Promise!" Jerald rubbed her face with affection. "I miss you too, baby! Now that Justin will be living with us permanently, we'll have more time to spend together as a family. And...once he is settled in, I will make arrangements for you to meet Keisha. How does that sound?"

"Sounds like a plan." Ada's face lit up.

"The only debate we should have for now on is how the both of us can enhance our love for one another. Christ said to, 'Love your wife as He did the church, giving himself up'" [Ephesians 5:25]. He grabbed her, picking her up and gently swung her around.

"I love you Mrs. Ada D. Young. If the timing was right, I would take you with me. But I feel that you need to be home with our daughter. Trust me, I'll be fine! Now walk your husband out." He put her down and took her hand, passing between the couch, but not noticing Evie. Jerald opened the front door, leaving it ajar, he walked out. He chirps the alarm to his SUV, then turned around and gave his wife a medium-sized gift box with seven roses. Evie peeped out, making sure the coast is clear.

"Awe, Jerald! Thank you honey." Ada kissed him.

"You're welcome!" Jerald slightly closed the door.

"Open it inside once I'm gone! It will give you something to think about until I get back!" Jerald smiled.

11

A noise came from behind the front door. "Ouch." Evie stubbed her toe. "What was that?" Ada looked and paused for a moment. She looked in the house and seeing Evie's shadow through the cracked front door.

"I think someone has snuck out of bed again Jerald," Ada smirked. Jerald looked in the same direction, laughing while seeing Evie's shadow.

"Well let me go and I will give you a call once I get there," Jerald chuckled. Ada slightly laughed shaking her head. Jerald softly kissed her lips.

"Go put our daughter to bed!" Jerald kissed passionately. She watched Jerald's broad shoulders strut away from her, wishing he would change his mind and invite her along. He waved while getting into his eighteen-wheeler truck, blowing her one last kiss. Ada cracked a smile, and then walked toward the house feeling un-peaceful in her spirit.

"Evie Young, you have one second to get your happy behind back into bed now!" Ada gently scolds Evie as she approached the front door entrance. Evie ran up the stairs speedily from behind the front door; it swiftly slammed.

"I love you, Mommy," Evie sprints to the top of the stairs. Once she reached the top, Evie turned around, looked at her mom and smiled with an exit.

"Lord, what am I going to do with them both?" Ada shook her head. Evie walked back into her room and closed her door.

Chapter Two
An Unsolved Mystery

Evie's hotel room remained dark and cold. Darkness drifted in as the mystery of her life has yet to unfolded. Ten years of unanswered questions are still unsolved. Evie has become the victim of one man's disobedience.

Jerald thought Ada was jealous of Keisha. At one particular point in their marriage, that was the case. However, the last time the "Spirit of the God" really spoke through Ada. Jerald misjudged his wife's motives, which caused him to listen to the opposite voice.

Little did Evie know that the same deceiving voice that her father listened to, was the same deceitful voice hovering around her, patiently waiting to destroy her life!

◆◆◆◆◆

Evie's yellow school bus approached her house, she became excited. When the bus stopped, she could barely contain herself to get off.

"Torri, ask your mom could you come over so we can do our homework together and eat some of my mom's famous chocolate cookies?" Evie told Torri. The two young ladies walked towards Evie's house.

"Let me go home first and give my mom a kiss then I'll ask her." Torri looked at Evie with a smile.

"Cool. Justin should be home by now." Evie paused in thought.

"Hey, I have an idea!"

"What?" Torri waited for an explanation.

"You can help my dad and I unload Justin's things off his truck. Afterwards, he'll probably take us all to the ice-cream parlor."

"Yeah, that would be cool. I've always wanted to ride in an eighteen-wheeler," Torri spoke with excitement. The two ladies approached their houses.

"I don't see my dad's truck. He probably dropped Justin off at the house then went back to work." Evie noticed a strange white SUV in their driveway. "Whose truck is that?" Evie suspiciously asked herself.

 "Well, let me go and ask my mom. I'll come over if she says it's okay." Torri waved, then walked toward her red, brick house.

"Okay, see you later! I wonder whose truck this is," Evie continued to ask herself while walking up, two flights of brick stairs. The sun beamed on their stucco house. She walked inside to find her religious grandma standing over the stove; cooking something that smelled like a dead dog. Evie's cousin, who were old enough to be her father, laid slouched on the sofa. Ratchet music videos played on the television. The aroma of marijuana surrounded the room.

"Where is my mother?" Evie questioned her Grandma Ann.

"Where are your manners?" That's no way for an eight-year-old to enter a house!" Grandma Ann rolled her eyes. Evie rolled her eyes into the back of her head while sucking her

teeth. "Hello Grandma Ann, now where is my mother?" Evie anxiously questioned.

"I never did like you or your smart mouth!" Grandma Ann ranted.

"Your mother went somewhere hours ago, and I don't know when she's coming back! I know how your mother used to be. She pretends to be so godly, faithful, and loyal to your father, but she has hidden secrets. She thinks no one knows about them, but I certainly do!" Grandma Ann blurted out.

"I ought to . . . Whoo!" Evie angrily balled up her fist, and left the kitchen, stomping her size four shoes. She marched upstairs to her bedroom, murmuring.

"You're lucky you are my grandma, old ugly unhappy want-to-be Christian hound!" Evie frowned with wrinkles on her forehead. Evie began to sing, while throwing her white, bone, and beige-colored stuffed animals across her bed. She accidentally fell asleep at the foot of her bed, waiting for her parents to return.

Darkness sets in Evie's room. She turned over wiping the drool from her mouth, opening her right eye, and then the left. She woke up from her nap, sliding herself into an upright position on her bed. Evie turned on the lamp, and then turned around to look at her bedroom door. Raising her feet, she walked over to the silver doorknob and opened the door, and then stared across the hall into Justin's room. His room still looked the same way before she fell asleep.

"Maybe Justin and Momma are playing cards downstairs like always." Evie walked down the carpeted steps. She headed toward the end of the stairwell. Looking into the kitchen, she sees no one. With curiosity, Evie walked into the living room to the same old

nightmare that caused her to fall asleep in the first place. Grandma Ann! Puzzled, Evie looked at the ancient clock on their wallpapered living room wall.

"It's almost midnight! Where is everyone?" Evie worried with an uneasiness. Grandma Ann fell asleep on the sofa. Her snore overpowered the volume of the TV. Rolling her eyes, Evie shook her.

"Grandma, wake up. Where is my mother?" Evie continued to nudge her. Grandma Ann wiped her mouth and looked rather astonished at Evie.

"What time is it?" Grandma Ann questioned Evie.

"It's time for you to tell me where my mother is! I haven't seen her all day. Where is she? This is not like her!" Evie demanded answers. Grandma Ann slowly sat up on the sofa, then stood in front of Evie. Immediately raising her hand, she slapped Evie across the left-side of her face. Evie's honey-brown face turned red.

"Don't you ever speak to me in that tone! Who do you think you are?" Grandma Ann walked toward the kitchen. Evie stood still with tears in her eyes, holding her face.

"I'll take your little tail and beat you like I used to do your sorry mother.

You'll mess around and get locked in the basement until your parents get back! You got the wrong one little girl!" Grandma Ann yelled, and then walked to the kitchen to wash her hands.

"You are just like that damn Ada for the world. Like mother, like daughter! Take your tail back upstairs! I told you before your mother isn't here!" Grandma Ann rants turning off the water faucet and reached for a hand towel.

"I didn't eat dinner!" Evie spoke with pain in her voice.

"And you're not going to eat!" Grandma Ann opened the refrigerator door.

Evie marched up the carpeted stairs like a soldier. She entered into her bedroom and slammed the door. A picture of an African goddess queen painted in red, yellow, and white in a gold picture frame hits the floor. Evie angrily sat on the bed and folded her arms. Tears flooded her face.

"I should go back downstairs and beat her in the head with a hammer!" Evie thought to herself; she broke down in tears.

"I will comfort little hearts when mommies can't. I will protect you from wolves when they are amongst you. And I will give you rest when your heart is heavy." The Spirit of God comforted.

"God, what happened to my mom? Did something happen? Is she coming back, or do I have to stay with this witch for the rest of my life? She'll beat me to death and then feed me to the dogs."

"Rest my little child, just rest." The Spirit Has Spoken. Evie pulled back her comforter with tears rushing down her eyes.

"My mommy always pulled my covers back just enough so it would be easy for me to make my bed in the morning. But now

she's not here to make sure I am doing it right. I don't care about tomorrow. I just want my mommy!" Evie vented, crying herself asleep. She turned off her light and slept in the dark without a night-light for the first time.

◆◆◆◆◆

Morning breaks, the sun beamed through Evie's window bright and clear. The sunshine alarmed her body to get up. She jumped to her feet, stretching, and realizing that it is the next day.

"Maybe today will be better than yesterday." Evie thought out loud. She ran to her bedroom door, swinging it open. Evie looked into Justin's reserved bedroom. But the only thing she saw was the same sign she made two days ago saying, "Welcome Home Justin." All of a sudden Evie began to hear voices coming from downstairs.

Her face lite up, "They're back!" Evie's joy deflated when she walked down the stairs, seeing her grandma, grandpa, uncle, Torri, Torri's Mom, distant relatives and two police officers. Evie stomped to the end of the stairwell, looking into the living room. At this point, Evie felt deep in her heart that her mom wasn't coming back, her dad went back to Keisha, his ex-wife, and Justin's coming to live with them was a lie!

The officer's walkie-talkie volume raised. He turned it down and walked toward Evie. She looked at him with her slanted watered brown eyes. He kneeled down to her level. Large teardrops fell from her eyes.

"My name is Officer Parks and that's Officer Randy." Officer Parks points to Officer Randy who stood in the livingroom speaking to Evie's grandparents. "What is your name little lady?"

"Evie Young," Officer Parks took Evie by her hand, and they

18

walked to the other side of the room, away from everyone else. "Evie I am afraid I have some bad news. Your mom left yesterday morning while you were in school. She told your Grandma Ann that she was going to look for your father because he had not called. She thought something had happened to him. No one has heard from her since. Unfortunately, your mom has not called or returned. So, we must write out a report stating that she has abandoned you." Officer Parks spoke with sincerity.

"My mom did not leave me here with that mean old lady. She loves me." Meanwhile, Officer Randy walked towards them, overhearing their conversation.

"There isn't a doubt in our mind Evie, that your mom doesn't love you." Officer Randy interrupted Evie and Officer Parks conversation.

"But the proof is she left you here, and since no one has heard from her . . ." Evie cried while Officer Parks silenced Officer Randy from finishing his sentence.

"Where's my father and brother? They're supposed to be here!" Evie asked. Officer Parks looked at Evie then sadly dropped his head.

"We have your father's information based on what your grandma gave us. Do you have or know any additional information that may help us search for your family?" Officer Parks looked at Evie with sympathy.

Evie looked up, slightly wiping her eyes. "I overheard my dad telling my mom that he was going to Delaware to pick up Justin, my stepbrother. He was bringing Justin back home to live with us permanently."

"Who does Justin live with right now?" Officer Randy questioned.

"His mother Keisha, my dad's ex-wife!"

Officer Randy looked at Officer Parks, slightly smiling at him.

"Okay Miss Evie. You have been a great help," Officer Parks pats Evie on her back.

"What's going to happen to me?" Evie wiped her eyes. "Please don't let me stay with that crazy woman! She is mean." Evie looked into the livingroom at Grandma Ann.

"She slapped me in my face last night and made me go to bed hungry. She hates my mother and me because we stopped going to her crooked religious church. So please Officer Parks, don't make me go with her. I'd rather go home with strangers!" Officer Parks kneeled down to Evie's level giving her a tissue from inside his shirt pocket.

"Officer Randy and I are going to make sure you are in good hands until your parents are found, okay?" Evie nodded her head while Officer Parks looked over into the living room at Grandma Ann. Both Officers walked to the other side of the kitchen away from Evie.

"Where's the kid going?" Officer Randy inquired in his Italian accent.

"Too bad Kathy and I are unable to keep her until her parents retuned. She's a sweet girl."

"Chief John would not grant you the privilege," Officer Randy replied in jealousy.

"It was just a thought." Officer Parks responded, looking at Evie with sympathy.

"I'm telling you her father probably didn't know how to tell Evie's mom that he was going back to his ex-wife. You hear stories like this all the time."

"And how do you know that?" Officer Parks questioned Officer Randy, displaying a puzzled expression on his face.

"Come on! It's obvious and you know it!" Officer Randy looked at officer Parks.

"No! I don't and neither do you!" Officer Parks firmly stared.

"Come on Parks, you see those 'love and hate movies' on how they leave their . . ." Officer Parks interrupted.

"Excuse me, Randy. With all due respect, you're accusing Evie's dad of going back to his ex-wife without proof, and I will not stand here and entertain your negative thoughts!" Officer Parks looked at him with a straight face.

"Just put yourself in Evie's shoes and feel the hurt that this little girl feels. The only thing she remembered is her parents telling her they'll be back and then all of a sudden they disappeared without a trace!" Officer Parks addressed in a low stern tone.

Officer Randy walked away to join the rest of the family in the

living room. Officer Parks walked toward Evie, who was sitting at the bottom of the stairs. Evie's heart felt as though it is going to fall out from the pain she was feeling. Evie looked up to Officer Parks standing in front of her.

"Okay Evie. Come with me. We are going into the living room, and we are going to make sure you are placed somewhere safe until we help find your parents." Officer Parks reassured.

"Put her into foster care." The Spirit spoke to Officer Parks.

"No don't put her in foster care. Whatever relative agrees to take her, let them take her," spoke another voice.

Evie stood up, taking Officer Parks' hand, and she dragged her feet into the living room. "May I have everyone's attention please?"

"Obviously, the parents of Evie Young are currently missing. You all are her closest relatives and Evie's grandmother stated earlier that Evie could not stay with her." Grandma Ann gave Evie a mean look and then smiled at Officer Parks with a wink.

 "There are two options. It's either going to be a family member having temporary custody of Evie until this case is resolved, or we have to call social service to come pick the child up. From there, she will be placed in foster care." He looked down at Evie sympathetically giving her a gentle smile. Her best friend Torri stood with her mother, nudging her.

"Hey, Mom. Can Evie come and live with us, can she? It'll be cool! I can be the big sister she's never had!" Torri suggested.

"Honey, I know Evie is your best friend and I love her as my own.

But I don't think that's a good idea for us to get involved. Let's just let her stay close to her immediate family until her mom comes back. I am pretty sure there is a legitimate explanation for why Ada left and hasn't come back yet." Torri's mom grabbed Torri by the hand. "Come on honey it's time for dinner." They both walked off, looking at Evie.

"I have to go home Evie." Torri eyes began to water with tears as she stared at Evie. Torri hugged Evie as if it was the last time, she would see her.

"Goodbye." Teardrops fell from Torri's eyes. Evie began to cry harder.

"Maybe she needs to be in foster care," replied Evie's grandmother. Officer Parks stared at Grandma Ann, holding back what was on his mind. His thoughts were to take her to jail for child abuse. He continued to stare. Finally, someone stepped forward. "We will take her!"

"And you are?" Officer Parks questioned.

"I'm Tammy Wilks and this is my husband, Gene. I'm Evie's aunt, Ada's sister." Tammy looked at Officer Parks. She scratched in between her tracks.

"My husband and I live in Savannah, Georgia. "I'm a nurse and my husband is an engineer. Evie will be well taken care of!" Before they could finish Evie interrupted. "She is a pure stranger to the family. I don't know her or him. I've seen them maybe once or twice, but they are strangers to me. My mother doesn't even talk to her. Please, I don't want to go to Savannah with them. It's too far, and it's away from everybody, especially my best friend." Tammy looked at Evie.

"We own a six-bedroom house, and you can have the largest room, Evie.

"Mrs. Wilks do you and Mr. Wilks have any children?" Officer Parks questioned her.

"No... we don't! But hopefully one day we will. We've been trying but I guess the time isn't right!" Officer Randy walked over toward Officer Parks with the finished paperwork.

"So let me ask you, what makes you capable of taking care of Evie until Mr. and Mrs. Young returns?" Officer Parks anticipated an answer.

"She's my niece, and I love her! I will treat Evie as if she was my very own daughter!"

Officer Parks took Evie by the hand. "Come with me and let's have a talk, little lady."

"Officer Randy, can you go over the procedures with the Wilks so we can wrap this up?" Officer Parks instructed. Officer Randy slightly nodded his head, and then walked across the room toward the Wilks.

"Evie, your dad and I have been friends for a very long time and we're going to do everything that we can to find him. In the meanwhile, I think it's a good idea for you to go stay with your aunt. And if I could take you with me I would, but I can't. Your grandma doesn't want you, and I am glad she doesn't." Evie made a sadder face as Officer Parks reiterated his comments with a stutter.

"What I meant by saying that was, I would rather that you went with another family member instead of her. I feel that you would be safer if you went with your Aunt Tammy and Uncle Gene. They may be strangers to you, but in foster care you'll be around children and people who are more than strangers! So, what do you say?" Evie hunched her shoulders.

"Whatever!" Evie answered with an attitude, then stood up and stomps her feet up the stairs. The family watched Evie storm to the top of the stairs. She entered her room and slammed the door behind her. Officer Parks placed his hand over his forehead in distressed.

"As of this date you have temporary guardianship over Evie Young." Officer Randy went over the procedures of the temporary agreement.

Officer Parks walked over to Officer Randy and the Wilks. "In thirty days, if Evie's parents haven't shown up, you must report it to the courts in Savannah Georgia. They will then set up a hearing and just let them know whether or not you would like permanent custody." Stated Parks.

"Will do." Tammy agreed.

Evie's grandma and the rest of the people in the Young's house began to leave. "Here are the keys to lock up. Oh, and Tammy, thank you again for coming to get Evie." Grandma Ann exited out the front.

"By ma!" Tammy rolled her eyes with a reply. Officer Parks walked back over to the Wilks handing them papers to sign. As the decision-making wrapped up, Evie packed her clothes in a red roller suitcase. She ran across some pictures from their vacation.

It was one with Justin and her sitting at a small restaurant table. Another one with her holding her signature basketball from one of the NCAA Women's Leagues. And the last one with Justin wearing Mickey Mouse ears from Disney World. Evie smiled as she looked at a picture she had taken with her parents. Tears began to roll down her face. Evie got on her knees and prayed.

"Dear God, I miss my mommy and daddy. I ask you to bring them back. My heart hurts. I want them home with me. Do they love me anymore? Does my dad still love my mom? Did he go back to Keisha? Please God, answer my prayers." Aunt Tammy and Gene walked into Evie's bedroom finding her in tears on her knees.

"Come on Evie all the paperwork has been completed. Don't worry about your clothes. You'll get new ones tomorrow." Aunt Tammy demanded. "You can leave that old stuff here! "Evie looked at them silently. She stubbornly zipped her suitcase closed, stood up and rolled it to the front and exited.

"I already see we are going to have problems with this girl!" Gene told Tammy as they watched Evie walk down the stairway. Tammy shook her head. At the bottom of the stairs, Evie looked into the vacant living room. Gene and Tammy walked past Evie and opened the front door. Gene goes to the car, grabbing Evie's suitcase. Tammy waited for Evie at the front door holding it open. "Today please," Tammy sarcastically spoke.

"This is going to be a long, horrible drive!" Evie mumbled to herself as she walked to the Wilks luxury car. "If I had the guts, I would kill myself right now!" Evie thought. She opened the backdoor, looking at her beautiful beige and brown stucco home. "I hope I see you again?" Evie took one last look, and then closed her eyes. She cuddled up on the leather back seat. The car pulled out of the driveway and off on the journey.

Chapter Three
Deception Leads

After a long fifteen-hour drive from Poughkeepsie, New York to Savannah, GA, Evie thought they would never get there. Aunt Tammy laid on her arm asleep while leaned against the glass window on the passenger's side. Gene drove the car inside their garage. He placed the gear in park; the car slightly jerked, awakening Tammy.

"We're here!" Gene informed. Evie frowned.

"Yeah, we're here alright!" Evie mocked him under her breath. Gene looked at Evie in the rearview mirror, while he opened his car door.

Tammy jumped out of the car yelling, "I'll meet you two inside. I have to pee!" She rushed through the entrance of the house of the garage, leaving the house door open.

Gene opened the trunk from inside the car. It popped up. Evie looked around as her feet hit the cemented garage. She spotted a stuffed bull's head, hanging next to a brown handled sword. Gene walked toward the trunk. His beer belly hung in the way, as he picked up Evie's suitcase then hands it to her. Reaching for it, Gene then grabbed his wife's and his luggage. They both remained silent. Evie walked towards the door that was ajar. Gene slammed the trunk; he watched Evie's proportioned butt switch through her lilac, fitted sweatpants.

"That girl can't be eight with an ass like that! Good God Almighty!" Gene thought to himself as he flicked a toothpick in his mouth and struts his 6'6" football framed body behind her and

into the house. Tammy walked out of her bedroom onto the bone-colored carpet.

"Evie, you can bring your things upstairs. Let me show you your room." Tammy spoke from the balcony while looking down. Evie worked her way up the stairway.

"Nice room." Evie complimented, as she admired the lilac painting on the wall. The pretty dark purple and yellow border along the top, she stared at.

Evie walked toward another picture on the wall. "Who painted this?" The creative painting showed a brown swirl as a tornado and a woman lying in the sun on a lilac beach towel surrounded by tall trees. It had scattered green leaves all around.

"Oh, your mother!" Tammy responded in a jealous tone.

"Anyway, make yourself at home. Just don't mark up the walls or bring any food and drinks upstairs. I would like to keep this room clean, for the children I am waiting to have. If Gene stop going to sleep on me, maybe we can have some babies." Evie made a disturbing face while Tammy went on a rant.

"It's been a long drive so I'm going to the bar and get myself a drink. I'll be back later. Your uncle is grilling, so make sure he saves me some food. I know how that greedy hog eats. Just look at his stomach." Tammy laughed, walking out the bedroom.

"Great! I'm in the house with fatty and ALCHY!" Evie pitched her voice in a low sad tone.

28

"Such a beautiful view." Staring out the window Evie gazed at the tall trees and ten-acres of landed surrounded around the house.

"This is definitely a forest and county." Evie took a deep breath, flopping down on the bed, she propped her legs up and folded her arms. In tears, Evie broke down. Slouching, she pushed herself flat, and then placed the pillow over her face. The sun goes down, Evie fell asleep.

◆ ◆ ◆ ◆ ◆

Gene closed the screen door to the dark night. "It's almost 8:30. Let me go up here and see what this girl is up to." Gene placed the barbeque on the kitchen counter. He walked on the carpet barefoot. His calf muscles flexed on every step. Reaching the top of the stairs, he walked toward Evie's bedroom. Grabbed and turning the doorknob of her room, he called out, "Evie! Evie!"

The downstairs kitchen light gave him just enough glow. He walked toward the tall silver lamp, turning the knob dim. Gene walked to the door and peeked out. Turning his football neck left to right, and then closed the door. Quietly, he tipped toed towards Evie's bed while she laid on her stomach on the lilac comforter.

"Damn!" Gene grabbed his penis through his cut-off sweat shorts. He slipped his hand down his shorts and began to touch himself. He gazed at Evie's behind in the white cut-off shorts.

"Wake up." The angel softly whispered in her ear.

Evie opened her eyes. She stared at the window as she recognized that it's dark outside. "I don't remember leaving the lamp on." She thought to herself. Evie looked at the wall and saw a shadow. Immediately, she turned her body around to her uncle standing over her. He snatched his hand out of his shorts. Evie quickly balled her legs and grabbed a pillow, placing it toward her chest

29

firmly. "Oh, I didn't realize you were asleep. I was just coming to let you know that dinner is ready," Gene rubbed his head with the same hand that he caressed his manhood with.

"Why didn't you knock?" Evie stared for an explanation.

"Excuse me?! Did you just question me in my own house?! This is my house! I can do what I want; when I want!" Gene looked at Evie angrily. He then walked toward the exit door.

"No one told your momma to marry your sorry daddy. Now where is he? Probably in between the legs of his ex-wife!" Gene mumbled exiting.

Evie picked up a stuffed animal off the bed and threw it, hitting the bedroom door. She propped her legs up to her chin and started to bang her head into her knees.

"God, I don't want to be here." Tears rolled down her thighs like a troubled child sliding toward the deep end of a swimming pool.

◆ ◆ ◆ ◆ ◆

30 Days later . . .

Tammy left for work supposedly after dinner one day, but Evie knew where she was going.

"That woman is a witch from hell. I must have been drunk when I married her!" Gene chewed his food. Evie walked her plate to the sink and began to wash the dishes. He looked up, gazing at Evie's blue and white cotton fitted shorts. Gene ate the last spoonful of his macaroni and cheese while staring at Evie's back. Gene got up from the table, scrapped the excess food off his plate and into the

30

trash. Then he walked over to the sink. "Oh, excuse me," Gene brushed up against Evie's behind. She rolled her eyes and then began to wash the dishes quicky, until she accidentally broke a plate.

"Tammy is going to kill you if you keep breaking her plates!" Gene walked to the refrigerator and grabbed a beer. Evie quickly dried her hands, marched upstairs to her room and slammed the door.

"Bring your ass back here and sweep this mess up before I beat you like you stole something." Evie looked for a lock on the doorknob.

"Great, who makes knobs without a lock? Man!" Evie muttered with frustration and tears in her voice. She walked over and sat on the bed, then picked up the telephone and dialed. "God, please let my parents be back home," Evie spoke to herself.

"The number you have reached 212-555-0100 is no longer in service, please check the number and try your call again." The operator repeated. Evie slammed the phone down angrily and sighed. Hastily, she picked up the phone to dial her grandmother's number. Rolling her eyes; she took a deep breath.

"Hello!"

"Hi Granny, this is Evie. I know it's only been three days since I've last called. But I was just wondering if you've heard anything from my parents yet?"

"Look, why are you bugging the hell out of me?! Since you've been gone, you've called me way too much! Stop calling here! Just like I told you before you left home, and I'll tell you again, your daddy went back to his ex-wife! And your mother is roaming around like

31

a lost chicken with its head cut-off!" Evie laid the phone down on the nightstand, as her grandmother rants.

"That's what she gets. When any child young or old doesn't listen to their parents, bad things happen! Your father made you all leave our church just because he didn't like the way your grandfather and I were running things. Your mother never listened to nobody anyway! I told her not to marry that man, now look! That's what happens when you don't listen! God doesn't like ugly." Evie squeezed her eyes tight; tears pour down her face.

"You are going to be just like your mother!"

Evie hung up the phone and laid on her stomach pouring out her heart. Gene quietly stood outside of Evie's bedroom door eavesdropping.

"Oh, I think the baby needs some comforting," Gene gently opened the door gazing at Evie's body. Gene looked at Evie with lust in his eyes. He turned around and closed the door quietly. The loudness of her cry overpowered the sound of the closing door.

Gene walked over and stood at the foot of Evie's bed thinking about how good his niece's body would feel on top of his. Gene pulled down his sweatpants. Evie is unaware as she laid facedown crying into her pillow. Gene instantly pounced on her while putting his right-hand over her mouth. She lets out a weighted cry.

"I will kill you tonight if you move or cry out!" He whispered in her left ear while he pulled down her shorts. He paused for a brief moment, and then penetrated her.

"If you tell anyone about this, especially Tammy, I will kill you and

"Damn-it, Get up! Now!" Evie continued to lie there until Gene grabbed her by her curly hair.

"I hate hard-headed little girls. I said get up!" He pulled her up to her feet. Blood dripped down her thighs.

Evie managed to get enough strength to respond. "Yes sir." She drooped over. "That's better!" Gene lifted Evie's head up from her curly hair, he slapped her and then release her head, it drooped back down. "I like this fresh meat... oh yeah I can get use to this." Gene smiled while walking toward the exit.

"Welcome home! Tammy wants to stay in the streets, be my guest. I found something better to get into!"

◆ ◆ ◆ ◆ ◆

Gene continued to raped Evie for the next 8 years. Sexing his wife's niece became a day-to-day routine. As Evie's body began to develop, Gene began to get more pleasure out of her. He bought Evie whatever she wanted on a weekly basis. He also paid her $1,000 a week to stay quiet.

Gene began to manipulate Evie more and more until she began to enjoy having sex with him. Tammy's second home was the bar, so she knew nothing. When Evie got home from school, Gene rolled up a blunt and they smoked it together. Gene demanded Evie not to make any friends. His manipulative ways brain washed her into believing that he was her protector, and he was the only person she needed.

Chapter Four
The Escape

Gene consistently threatened Evie if she didn't have sex with him. Her fears caused her to give in. There were times when Gene entered into Evie's room in the middle of the night, forcing himself on her. Most of the times when Tammy got home, her drunkenness caused her to sleep straight through the night.

One early Tuesday morning, the birds chirped and praised God in the tall trees near Evie's window. She rolled over, frowned, and then balled herself into a knot from sharp stomach cramps. With all of her strength, Evie managed to slide her legs off the bed to pull back her lilac comforter. When she sat up, her feet barely touched the floor. She questioned herself on why she was in so much pain.

"Maybe too much sex." With a throbbing headache, Evie answered herself.

"And...too much weed." Evie laughed at herself, as her high cheekbone emphasized her slanted eyes.

"Ouch!" Evie held her stomach, trying to comfort her pain.

While holding her stomach, a huge, tall angel appeared, blinding her with an unbearable light. Evie held her right-hand up to her eye, trying to block the light.

"You will die tomorrow if you don't tell someone today about Gene. Be not afraid Evie. For the Lord has seen your innocent blood shed. But you will die if you fear."

The tall angel warned, and then the bright light faded away. Evie began to cry. When she uncovered her face, the angel was no longer there.

"Who can I tell? I can't talk to Tammy?" Evie spoke softly. "The police! But then if I do that, they'll put me in a foster home for sure. I am two years from being legal. That's okay." Evie shook her head to herself. She sniffled.

"If I can just make it to twelfth grade, I can then go to college far away from this psycho family." Evie figured this as her best plan.

"I wonder if I told Aunt Tammy, would she believe me? She already hates me. Too bad I didn't know all of this was going to happen. I would have begged Officer Parks to send me somewhere else." Spoke out loud.

"I don't believe that she pretended to be 'all sweet' in front of the officers." Evie continued to mumble, as the pain from her vagina reached her abdomen.

"Man! I feel like I'm going to die." Evie closed her eyes and rocked back and forth in the white cotton sheets.

"Okay, Evie! What are you going to do? If I stay here, I will die, so I will go ahead and tell Aunt Tammy. After all, what else could happened that hasn't? Evie stood on her feet trying to bare the pain. Her left-hand helped push her body up off the bed and onto her feet. She walked to the cherry wood dresser and looked in the mirror.

"God, at one time I felt so beautiful." Evie recalled as she pulled out a pair of jeans and a red shirt. She looked in the mirror and began to run her fingers through her tangled curly hair.

36

"Ouch!" her finger pulled out some of the knots.

"That black nigga!" Evie noticed a huge dark red hickey on the right-side of her neck. Getting dressed, she walked to the door angrily. Evie gripped the doorknob, slanged the door open, and then stormed into Tammy's room.

As Evie walked by, she glared at Gene in the kitchen making his lunch through the balcony rails.

"Ass-hole!" Evie eyed him with attitude.

Aunt Tammy's bedroom door was opened. Evie walked in and closed the bedroom door behind herself. Standing in the doorway of the pale-yellow bathroom, Tammy curled her hair in the mirror.

"Good morning, Aunt Tammy." Evie boldly greeted. Her aunt holds the large curlers in an upright position on a small section of her hair. She turned her head, looking at Evie.

"Yes, good morning. Can I help you?" Tammy sarcastically answered.

"How was work last night?" Evie asked. She began to bite her nails.

"Why are you being nosey all of a sudden?" Tammy questioned as she puts down the curlers and picked up her clear rat tail comb.

"No other time do you come in this room and talk to me. So, what do you want and how much do you need?" Evie looked dropped

37

her head with fear in her eyes at Tammy's question. "Never mind." Evie began to walk away.

"No, she did not just ask me how much I needed!" Evie reflected in her thoughts.

"If only you knew how much your husband is taking out of your account to give me!" Evie sarcastically thought to herself. She stopped walking in her tracks.

"You will die, if you don't tell the truth." The angels voice echoed within. Evie. With urgency, she walked back into the bathroom.

"Remember, you said you wanted to die! Well, this is your opportunity. Besides, you're wasting your time! She's not going to believe you!" The evil voice spoke.

"I am a big girl! Whatever comes my way I can handle it." Evie reinsured herself. As she reached the bathroom and stopped, Evie stood in the same spot, she was in the first-time.

"Oh, it's you again! It must be a desperate need." Tammy styled her hair and grinned in sarcasm.

"As a matter of fact, it is a desperate need, Tammy! I need for you to hear what's been going on in this house for the past eight years."
Screamed! "You have never . . . ever . . . paid any attention to me! Why? You were too busy getting drunk!" Tammy slammed down her comb and turned towards Evie.

"The nerve of you!" Pointing her in Evie's face, Tammy stared in rage.

"I be damned, if I allow a sixteen-year-old to talk to me like she's, my momma! My own momma doesn't talk to me like that! And you want to disrespect me in my house! Get out! Now! It's time for you to go to school before you seriously get hurt little girl." Tammy resumed back into the mirror, fixing her bangs.

"No! I am not going anywhere until you listen to me!" Evie insisted with tears of hurt in her eyes.

"For eight years, Aunt Tammy! Eight! Whole! Long! Years!" Evie broke down in tears. They dripped down on the yellow bathroom rug.

"Uncle Gene rapped and have been having sex with me, from the time I got here!" Tammy dug into her make-up bag on the counter, taking out a foundation sponge.

"The first night I was here he came into my room and stood over me. There were times, he would rub up against my butt and stare at my breast while I watched TV in the living room. That's why I stayed in my room to avoid him." Evie poured out her heart while Tammy placed her brown foundation back into the bag. Taking out her chocolate lip-liner, she lined her lips.

"The night you told me to lie for you when Gene questioned whether or not you went to work, was the night he came upstairs to my room. Heavy tears interrupted Evie's story.

"I was lying on my stomach. He pounced on me, pulled down my shorts from the back and covered my mouth. He told me if I told anyone he would kill me! Your husband raped me Aunt Tammy! And, those sheets you were looking for, my blood got all over them. Gene threw them away and threatened me if I told you." Evie shared as her eyes filled with tears like crystal. Tammy stared

39

at Evie with a straight face. "You are a damn good liar! You are no better than my sorry ass. She used to lie to mama like that when she was your age. Now do you see where you get it from?" Tammy asked Evie as she rolled her eyes, putting her lipstick back into her make-up bag.

"How can you not believe me?! You think I would make this up? He snuck in my room Aunt Tammy when you were stone drunk or not home." Tammy began to shake her head back and forth.

"No...I don't believe you!" In disbelief Tammy fixed her lipstick.

"Your country ass husband forced me to get up and please him! He told me that his 'friend is lonely and needs a playmate. And if I didn't get up and play with him, he'd kill me!" Evie's voiced rage.

"He forced me to smoke weed with him!" Evie cried hysterically.
"Look at my neck! You see this hickey?!" Evie pulled her hair up, Tammy glanced.

"Your sick husband did this to your niece! He robbed me of my virginity! Maybe if you'd stayed home sometimes and out of the bars and acted like his wife, he'll have your ass to get into, instead of mines! I am not his wife! You are! Do you hear me?" Evie yelled.

Tammy turned around in Evie's face, picking up the hot curlers and slammed them down. Evie jumped!

"You are a disgusting whore! How dare you lie on my husband! Your doggish father disowned you and that pathetic sister of mine, who you called mother! He didn't want you or her in the first place! Jerald was supposed to be my husband, and your desperate

mother stole him from me!" Tammy yelled. "Since we were kids, Ada has been crazy! So, I kept my distance. The only reason I came to rescue you is because granny called me, saying that you were getting out of hand. She was tired of you. Your mother probably wanted to give you away after realizing your daddy didn't want her any longer!" Evie stood in front of Tammy devastated, as tears ran down her face.

"But I stepped in and claimed you. Now I regret it! You're nothing, just as your mother is nothing!" Evie balled her fist in fierce. Tammy looked down at Evie's hand. "What, you want to fight me?" Tammy asked in rage. Pulling Evie by her long curly hair, she punched her in the eye. Evie reached for the hot curlers. With all of her might, she swung hitting Tammy in the head. Aunt Tammy screamed from the burn and force, and then fell out.

Tammy hits the floor cold. Gene heard the noise from downstairs. He rushed upstairs and into the bathroom. Evie flied past him, giving him an angry look.

Evie rushed into her bedroom and began to pack. "I got to get the hell out of here." Evie squatted down on the side of the bed, reaching for her red roller suitcase. Her eye began to swell. Evie looked under the bed for her shoes and found a 45-chrome caliber.

"Oh ... my ... God! So, he was planning on killing me." Evie examined the gun. Her eyes and mouth widen. She looked at the door of her room, then back to the gun.

"How do I open this thing?" She questioned herself, trying to remember how her dad taught her to load a gun for hunting. Evie closed the loaded gun and laid it in the corner of her suitcase. Voices came from out in the hallway. Quickly Evie threw her clothes inside the suitcase and zipped it up.

"Take the gun out of your suitcase and put it in your side pocket." The angel spoke. Evie quickly obeyed. When Evie reached the exit, she placed her suitcase down and opened the door to Gene and Tammy standing side-by-side.

"We knew you were going to try and run away." Tammy stated with a huge burnt knot on her forehead. "Now what is this you've told my wife about me? I did not molest or rape you. You came in and pushed yourself on me. Isn't that right Evie?" Evie gave Gene a mean eye.

"Get out of my way!" Evie demanded as Gene and Tammy remained still blocking her exiting.

"I told her she's a liar, just like her mother," Tammy committed.

"Talk about my mother one more time? She's not here to defend herself, so I will! Now, just like I said before, get out of my way. NOW!" Evie screamed.

"Girl you better . . ." Tammy attempted to threatened her, until Evie interrupted Tammy with a gun pointed in both their faces.

"OR WHAT?!" Evie boldly questioned.

"Yeah Gene, only stupid people leave their guns lying around. So, this is how you were going to kill me?! When were you planning on doing it Gene? When you're stroking me from behind or when I'm down on my knees?" Evie pointed the gun to the middle of Gene's eye.

"Don't even think about it Tammy." Evie warned her as she looked from her peripheral view. Evie's stepped back pointing the 45 at

them both. "ANSWER ME!" Evie yelled in his face. "When were you planning on killing me?" Evie stomped on his toes.

"Ouch!" Gene moaned and then silenced himself. Evie looked at him, while she cocked the gun. "Get down know, the both of you!" Gene and Tammy got on their knees with their hands in the air.

"I wasn't trying to kill you." Gene answered with fear in his voice.

"How did this gun get under my bed??" Evie questioned.

"I don't know!" Gene sternly replied.

"Oh, you don't know now!" Evie slightly laughed while walking behind him. She grabbed him by the throat, pointing the gun in his nostril.

"How does it feel when someone else is in control? Huh Gene?" Evie asked as she pressed the gun further into his nose. Gene squinched his eyes. Evie switched her focus to Tammy. She walked to her pointing the shiny gun tip towards Tammy's mouth and keeping her eyes on Gene.

"Open it!" Evie demanded. Tammy refused. The wrinkles on Tammy's forehead displayed as she frowned. Evie smacked Tammy in the mouth with the gun. Tammy opened her bloody mouth. Evie placed the gun in it. Blood dripped running down Tammy's chin and onto the carpet.

"And you Tammy . . . you have the nerve to call me a whore?! I told you that your husband raped me. And you called me a liar! I ought to shoot you right now! Tammy looked into Evie's swollen eye that's almost shut.

"Look Tammy! You have blood all over the carpet." Evie took the bloody gun tip out of Tammy's mouth and wiped it all over Gene's white collared shirt. Steam of rage displayed in his eyes.

"You like blood so much...here, wear your wife's for a change!" Evie grabbed her suitcase as Gene and Tammy remained at gun point.

"Do not shoot them, just use the weapon to escape." The angel reminded Evie.

"No! Go ahead and shoot them. Look at what they did to you." The evil voice replied. "Get up!" Gene and Tammy stood up, as Evie nudged them both in the back with the tip of the gun and pushed them into the hallway.

"Since I've moved here you both have traumatized me, including your ugly mother." Evie stared at Tammy upon her statement. I have never in all my life been so torn, confused, violated and hurt!" Evie yelled.

"I am only sixteen and I have already experienced life at it's worse. You both were supposed to protect and love me as your own. Instead, you've abused me in every way! You both are sick! Evie yelled. Tammy wiped her mouth as tears fell from her eyes.

"So, I am giving you both warning right know!" Evie spoke in authority, wiping the tears from her eyes.

"I will kill you and then call the cops and turn myself in if you don't move out of my way! Trust me when I say, you will never see or hear from me ever again, believe that!" Evie emphasized.

"You have ruined my life and I HATE BOTH OF YOU!" Evie screamed at the top of her lungs. "NOW... MOVE... THE HELL... OUT OF MY WAY!" Fiercely Evie stared at them both. Gene and Tammy stepped aside. Evie tossed her suitcase down the stairs, it tumbled, as it hits the wall leaving a mark. Evie walked down the carpeted stairs, backwards while pointing the gun at Gene and Tammy.

"Can I have my gun back?" Evie laughed at Gene' requested.

"You're one stupid man!" Evie mocked Gene.

"Can I have my gun back!" She laughed.

"Why, so you can kill me because I didn't kill you both first? Then, you and Tammy will hide my body so no one will ever find me! I don't think so!" Gene placed his hand on the rail of the stairs.

"Your fingerprints are on that gun. If you get caught with it, you're going to jail!" Evie laughed at his statement.

"Not before you! It's your gun," Evie reminded. "Your fingerprints were on it first!" Grabbing the handle of the front door, Evie picked up her suitcase, and then exited. The door slammed.

"She better not ever let me see her alone in the streets." Tammy furiously stated while walking into her bedroom and slamming the door. Gene walked down the stairs steamed with anger. He opened the door quickly, looking around. Evie is nowhere to be found. Gene slammed the door and turned around marching back up the stairs.

Chapter Five
Ordered Footsteps

Evie ran down the busy streets of Savannah breathing heavy. In tears, she pulled her red suitcase alongside. She stopped at an intersection and noticed a large sign that displayed "Motel." Evie strolled across the crosswalk and headed towards the motel. A couple walked out the opposite door of the motel as Evie entered. They stared at Evie's eyes.

"It looks like someone got knocked the hell out!" Whispers and laughs, Evie ignored as she pulled the silver handle of the door with her right-hand, pushing her luggage in first. She walked to the front desk. Evie felt the swelling of her eye enlarging.

"How may I help you?" A middle-aged woman spoke as she sat on a high stool, staring at Evie's eye.

"I need a room please," Politely Evie requested. The lady gazed at Evie's eye. "And how much is it?" Evie questioned. The clerk looked down at a list on her desk and then back up at Evie.

"Are you okay?" The clerk asked with concern.

"Yes ma'am. I'm fine." Water formed in Evie's eyes like crystal, and the swollen eye dropped a tear down the right side of her face.

"Please ma'am. I am begging you. I have been through enough drama this morning with some crazy family members. I'll pay you whatever the cost is. But please can I have a room? I need to get ready for school."

Evie spoke firmly, trying to hold her tears back. "How old are you honey?" The clerk asked Evie.

"Sixteen." Evie answered.

"Jesus!" The clerk spoke sympathetically.

"You're just a baby." Evie placed her head down as she felt her eye tightening.

"Here sweetie!" The clerk typed on a white keyboard. Her red fingernails typed away, as she searched for an available room on the computer. She then stood up and went to the back and returned with a keycard in her hand. Walking back to the front, she passed it to Evie. The clerk frowned, and then began to pray in a language that sounded like Spanish to Evie. Evie looked at the clerk silently.

"She doesn't look Spanish to me, but she does sound like it." Evie thought to herself. The clerk lifted her head, staring at Evie.

"The Lord has a word for you." The front desk clerk leaned toward the window.
"I need to pray with you. The enemy has been assigned to destroy your life. It began when you turned eight. You were led astray.

But God is ordering your footsteps now. You must learn to hear His voice clearly and obey it. You are chosen by God." The clerk spoke putting her head down.

"Help lead her closer to Me by the order of My instructions. Don't address her by her name. Wait until she tells you. Her name is Evie. For she will think you are

47

one of her enemies and run away. Ask her name, and then she will tell you." The voice of God instructed.

"Are you okay?" Evie questioned the clerk who slowly lifted her head.

"What is your name?"

"Evie Young."

"I am Mrs. Klein." The clerk stated her name, who walked around her desk towards Evie. She extended her hand.

"Evie, I don't know you, but God does. He has ordered your footsteps. With you coming here, is not a coincidence. God asked me to pray a prayer of protection around you. Can you take my hand?" Mrs. Klein gently asked as both ladies joined hands. Mrs. Klein prayed.

"Father we come before you in the name of Jesus on this day. We ask that your 'Divine Protection' surround Evie. I command her angels to go forth, right now in the name of Jesus, protecting her from all harm and danger of the enemy. Let Evie know that you love her and that it was you that protected her today and spared her life. Father, I thank you for ordering her footsteps daily in Jesus' name, Amen!"

"Amen!" Evie agreed with the clerk. Mrs. Klein gave Evie a hug and walked back behind the counter. She reached into her red purse pulling out a brochure about some church information.

"Here, this is for you. If you need any more information, my husband and I will be honored to serve you." Evie glanced at the brochure, and then looked up at Mrs. Klein.

"What is the charge for the room?" Evie inquired.

"There isn't one. God is going to take care of you. Just obey His voice when He speaks." Mrs. Klein replied with a smile.

"Thank you so much!" Evie showed appreciation and smiled.

"You're very welcome and your room is three doors down on the right. Room 173. And one other thing." Mrs. Klein spoke as she walked to the back office. Evie looked at the clock on the wall as the clerk disappeared out sight.

"Please hurry! I don't want to be late." Evie thought to herself while Mrs. Klein walked toward her.

"Here! I know you have to get to school but for about 10 minutes or so, place this ice pack on your eye. There's a little refrigerator in your room. You can place it in the freezer, in that way you'll have it when you come back." Mrs. Klein instructed as she smiled at Evie.

"Thank you." Evie smiled back and grabbed her things.

"Ouch! "She placed her right hand over her swollen eye. As Evie approached the door, she placed the keycard into the key slot and pulled it out. The door opened, Evie entered, and locked it. Inside, she leaned up against the door, fell to her knees, and bursts out in tears. She cried, her swollen eye became tighter and tighter. Evie crawled wailing toward the mirror.

She jumped up and screamed. "Oh my God!" Evie placed the ice pack on the table and fell back to the floor. The more she cried out, the more her swollen eye throbbed with pain.

49

"I can't go to school looking like this." Evie thought to herself while she placed her hand near the swollen eye.

 "If I skipped school until the swelling goes down, my grades will drop."

"I can't miss school. It won't look good on my records for college," Evie pondered as she stood up and walked toward her suitcase. Squatted down and unzipped it.

"Maybe I can play it off by wearing sunglasses." She rambled in the side pocket of her suitcase and took out a pair of black shades. She placed them on, stood up and walked toward the mirror again.

"Yeah! That looks good!" Evie fixed her curly black hair with her fingers while looking in the mirror. Evie reached into the pocket of her sweatpants for a hair scrunchy and placed it in a ponytail. She walked toward her luggage and grabbed something to wear.

After pulling out a pair of denim jeans and a white short sleeved shirt, Evie entered into the bathroom, closed the door, and undressed.

"If I could take off my entire body this easy and start all over again from birth, life would be grand!" Spoke aloud. "But, too bad I can't! God gave me sense of feel and this hurts!" In tears, Evie turned on the hot water and got into the shower. The steam began to rise, she closed the shower curtain and watched the unclean water go down the drain.

◆ ◆ ◆ ◆ ◆

Mrs. Klein sat at her desk having a conversation with God.

50

"Lord, what happened to that baby?"

"All things will be revealed to you. Be patient." The Spirit of God replied. Mrs. Klein sat back in her chair, closed her eyes, and folded her arms. Taking a deep breath, she exhaled slowly and entered into deep thought about her own daughter who the enemy is slowly destroying.

"Ma'am." A strange man called from the window. Mrs. Klein was in a deep daze that made her unaware.

"Excuse me, ma'am!" The strange man called her again. He balled his fist up and banged on the window. Ma'am!" He called louder. Mrs. Klein finally opened her eyes to a mean look

"Oh! I apologize sir! I didn't know you were standing there." Mrs. Klein stood.

"You should be!" Rudely the strange man spoke. "If you stop sleeping on the job, maybe the parking lot would be full!"

He remarked. "Who's your boss? You need to be reported."

"Jesus!" Mrs. Klein replied with a smile! The strange man waved his hand in frustration.

"Whatever! Jesus ain't got nothing to do with you sleeping on the job!"

"Actually, I wasn't asleep. I was praying. But please forgive me for not acknowledging you right away!" Mrs. Klein sincerely apologized.

"Now, what can I do for you sir?"

"Man!" The strange man waved his hand in frustration, and then exited the lobby. Mrs. Klein smiled with a sigh.

◆ ◆ ◆ ◆ ◆

Mrs. Thompson stood before her class reviewing the history lesson for the day. She looked at Evie's empty desk.

"Has anyone seen Evie this morning?" She questioned her students. They looked around at each other, and shook their heads as a 'no,' while others shrugged their shoulders. Mrs. Thompson walked away from the chalkboard, stretching her light brown legs toward her desk.

She fixed her clothes as she sat down in her rolling chair. "Let me go ahead and take attendance." When I call you name, raise your hand?" Mrs. Thompson instructed with a pencil in her hand. She called out names and roamed her eyes back and forth from the paper to the students. Evie ran into classroom door upon her name called. She sat down at her desk in the back of the classroom.

"You're late Miss Young. Do you have a late pass?" Mrs. Thompson asked. In the silent room, Evie walked up to Mrs. Thompson's desk as students looked at her up and down. Evie placed a white slip, on Mrs. Thompson's desk.

"And please take your shades off in my class?" Mrs. Thompson asked Evie as she walked back to her desk. She sat down.

"I can't do that!" Evie replied while looking down at her desk. She then lifted her head while looking at Mrs. Thompson.

52

"Excuse me!" Mrs. Thompson expressed for an explanation.

"I just gave you an order and you are telling me you can't do that, and you're late. Report to the office now!" Mrs. Thompson pointed to the door, as her students whispered to each other.

"But Mrs. Thompson..." Evie tried to reason with her, but she is interrupted.

"End of discussion Miss Young!" Mrs. Thompson walked to the middle of the aisle. Without another word, Evie slammed her hand on her desk, pushing herself up. She looked at Mrs. Thompson through her shades then slung them off.

The glasses hit Mrs. Thompson in her stomach. "Oh my God!" Mrs. Thompson slowly spoke while placing her right-hand over her mouth.

"I bet she feels really stupid!" Evie's classmate commented while Mrs. Thompson looked sadly at Evie.

"What happened to your eye?" Mrs. Thompson asked softly as Evie angrily looked at her. Voices came from all areas of the room. Evie silently looked at her sternly. Without a blink, she walked to Mrs. Klein's feet and retrieved her sunglasses. Evie placed them back on in her teacher's face and quietly exited.

"Class, finish reading chapter six until I get back." Mrs. Thompson instructed her class. Quickly Mrs. Thompson took long strides toward the exit. She ran down the hallway in her high heels to catch up with Evie, who Evie approached the end of the hallway. Mrs. Thompson called out her name, Evie ignored.

Evie began to run toward the stairwell. Mrs. Thompson sprinted down the hallway toward the exit of the first floor. Mrs. Thompson ran down the stairs and grabbed Evie by her arm from behind. Evie swung herself around, facing Mrs. Thompson.

"Who did this to your you?" Mrs. Thompson questioned. She then took off Evie's sunglasses. Evie snatched them back, while looking at Mrs. Thompson angrily through one eye.

"Oh, now you're concerned!" Evie responded while releasing an angry laugh. "It's sad Mrs. Thompson! It's like you tell people things and they don't believe you! And the people who do believe 'every word you say' are nowhere to be found. So, tell me teacher, what's a person supposed to do?" Evie sarcastically questioned. "Take a chance with those who 'may believe you' and accept it when they don't!" Evie answered her own question as she shook her head silently.

"Evie, I apologize! When a teacher's 'A' student, who is also her quietest student at that, comes into class late and is wearing sunglasses, is concerning! But I should've recognized that something wasn't unusual." Mrs. Thompson gently addressed.

"Now are you going to tell me who did this to you? Evie smiled and paused while looking down at Mrs. Thompson's shoes. Evie resumed her eyes back at her teacher.

"I fell off my uncle's motorcycle when I was riding. He was going too fast. I fell on my face, and then he fell on me from behind!" Evie sarcastically responded.

"He tried to teach me how to ride, but I guess I was too young to handle it! In the process of it, I got hurt really bad!" Evie responded with a smirk.

Putting her shades back on, Evie walked down the hallway. Mrs. Thompson looked at Evie dumb founded as the bell rung. Mrs. Thompson remained standing in the middle of the stairwell. The noises from loud students surrounded her, while Evie walked back up the stairs. Evie reached the second-floor landing and walked down the hallway toward her second period class.

"One thing I learned from Jesus is parables! It throws stupid people off." Evie thought to herself with a smile. She approached the doorway of her class and looked back down the hallway.

Chapter Six
God's Plan, Satan's Trap

Evie continued her day in school being humiliated and embarrassed. Due to school rules, students weren't allowed to wear sunglasses in school. That left Evie exposed to the disaster in her life with the shame of a swollen eye for all to see. After seventh period, the dismissal bell rang. Evie walked through the hallway with her arms folded around her two books. Other students walked in groups whispering to one another about her eye.

"People these days don't care and neither do I." Evie thought to herself, as she walked to her locker and turned the combination to her lock.

"I hate Mrs. Thompson! I hate this school and I hate my stupid life." Evie mumbled, taking out her book bag, stuffed her books in it, and then slammed the locker door. Evie walked down the hallway with anger raging through her entire body.

"Damn... who knocked you out?" Three boys commented, as she walked past them, headed towards an exit door. Evie glanced at the boys with a mean face. Unzipping the front compartment of her book bag, she pulled out her shades and put them on. Walking down three flights of stairs; she took off running like a supercharged sports car. Down the stairs and around the corner, Evie ran. Her book bag swung back and forth across her shoulder. She reached the end of the stairwell and swiftly ran out.

"I don't believe I've been left in this world to fight alone! Maybe I should run into this wall, so my brains can scatter!" Evie pondered in her mind as she ran along the side of a tall, red brick apartment

building. And she ran... tilting her head, closer and closer to the wall. Evie screamed to herself, breathing heavy and holding her stomach through her white shirt. Falling to her knees, Evie looked up ahead towards the end of the block.

"If I can only make it down this street." She spotted the motel sign with sharp pains that went through her abdominal area.

"Honey are you alright?" A middle-aged woman inquired, as she opened her car window. The woman stepped out of the white, mid-sized vehicle and walked toward Evie. She squatted down in front of her.

"I'm fine." Evie responded while slowly getting up. The woman looked at her.

"Are you sure you're okay, and what happened to your eye?" The woman dressed in denim jeans and a striped shirt asked as she helped Evie stand.

"Didn't I say I'm fine?" Evie snapped.

"I was just trying to help you." The lady insisted.

"And thank you, but I don't need help! Hopefully it's just my cycle trying to come on." Evie replied as the woman interrupted her.

"Hopefully! You're only but what, sixteen, seventeen?" The lady questioned. Evie gazed into the woman's eyes as she stood up and walked away. The lady walked back to her vehicle. Evie turned her head forward the lady, she looked at Evie and shook her head.

"She probably played hooky and some boy beat her up, old fast tail!" The lady assumed driving off.

Evie turned her head backwards, looking at the lady drive off in the opposite direction. While she dug into her tight denim pocket for her room card, she placed her left hand over her mouth walking up to the door. Fumbling, she pushed the keycard in at the key slot and quickly pushed the door open. Vomit dripped through her hand. She kicked the door shut with her right foot, dropped her bookbag down and ran into the bathroom. Falling on her knees, Evie vomited with her face in the toilet. She flushed, and then grabbed some toilet tissue and wiped her mouth. Evie stood up and looked herself in the mirror. With all of her might, she smacked the glass with her hands in anger.

"God! I hate you! Why did you let this happen to me?" She screamed at the top of her lungs.

"I thought I was your little girl. Look at me!" Evie ranted as she slapped the mirror again and walked out of the bathroom. Tears saturated her cheeks. She grabbed her suitcase and placed it on the bed. Evie sat to the left of it, opened it and dug in the sides. She pulled out a small black calendar and began to count the days.

"No...no! My period is late." Evie slapped her thigh in frustration.

Evie placed the calendar between her and the suitcase, taking out three pairs of white, balled up ankle socks. She unfolded the first pair, and then pulled out a black velvet diamond pouch. Evie placed the unfolded sock on the side of her; she counted $15,000 in $100 bills. Evie laid the money on the red and white flowered comforter. Picking up the next sock, she counted one-hundred $50 bills. There's a knock at the front door. Evie looked at the door quickly, when a second knock occurred. Evie stood up, turned around and placed her suitcase on top of the cash, and

then walked toward the door. She peeked through the curtains, and then opened the door.

"Hi Evie, did I disturb you?" Mrs. Klein smiled at Evie.

"Actually, you did!" Evie hesitantly stated, scratching her scalp. Mrs. Klein looked at Evie with a smirked. "I just wanted to check on you."

"I'm fine! Thank you." Evie smiled and closed the door. Mrs. Klein looked at the closed door, and then headed toward the office.

"Lord, how would you like me to help Evie?" Mrs. Klein questioned the Spirit of God.

"Treat her as you would treat your daughter Sheila." Mrs. Klein stopped walking as she listened to the Spirit of God. She sadly placed her left-hand over her mouth while the Spirit instructed her.

Meanwhile, Evie staggered back to the bed. She lifted her suitcase off the cash and placed it aside. As she gathered her hard-earned money, Evie became nauseated. Throwing the money on the bed, she ran into the bathroom and closed the door. Vomit went everywhere.

The eight years Gene raped and pimped his niece, Evie made a total of $60,000 and managed to save $20,000 of it. It's a good thing she reserved funds for a rainy day.

◆◆◆◆◆

The sun peeked through the heavy drapes. Evie woke up and jumped out of bed in her white shorts and red tank shirt. Off to

the toilet she ran. "Blaargh!" Evie flushed; grabbing toilet tissue, and then wiped her mouth. Once she finished vomiting her insides out, she walked away from the toilet and looked in the mirror, touching her swollen eye.

"You're pregnant." Evie's intuition spoke.

"No!" Evie cried, pulling up her tank shirt. She looked at her belly, placed both hands on her ears and shook her head in disbelief.

"I am not pregnant!" Evie believed, walking away from the mirror and went back into bed.

All morning, Evie had experienced symptoms of pregnancy. While lying in bed, she continued to hear her inner voice speak.

"You're pregnant!"

Evie skipped school that day and bought a pregnancy test. Once she got back to her room, she took the test. Positive it is! She found a local clinic nearby to check-in for a checkup. Once her examination was completed, Evie exited the room in anguish.

"Fifteen weeks pregnant! This is a freaking nightmare! A baby...by my uncle!" Evie cringed and shook her head in complete shock. She walked to the receptionist's desk where the examiner had left her file.

"Excuse me?" The receptionist looked up while Evie's doctor walked past, smiled, and then disappeared down a hallway.

"Does this clinic do abortions?" Evie inquired.

"No. We don't, but I can give you a list that does." The receptionist handed Evie a paper, she looked at the list.

"Thank you," Evie smiled walking away.

Looking at the courtesy desk with a telephone up ahead, Evie walked towards it. She observed numerous of pregnant teenagers walking through the halls as she approached the telephone. Evie dialed. Looking at her plain fingernails, it rang.

"Yes, I would like to make an appointment." Evie looked around as she listened to the receptionist on the other end.

"My name is Evie Young. Yes, that's perfect! I'll be there tomorrow at 7 a.m. Thank you." Evie hung up the phone and walked through the front door of the clinic, towards the exit.

◆ ◆ ◆ ◆ ◆

Evie breathed heavy, running across the street, and then rushed to open her room door. Cupping the vomit in her mouth, she headed straight to the bathroom. The thought of murdering an innocent life sickened Evie's stomach. She grabbed a tissue and wiped her mouth .

"Why was I ever born?" Evie thought in distress.

"My life is no better than a pig's. Now, I have to live my life in my own vomit! Why do mothers have babies, just to leave them as bastards?" Evie wondered as she looked in the mirror and rubbed her stomach. She turned on the water in the bathtub to prepare herself for the next day, thinking about the murderer she was about to become. Evie left on her panties and bra on, as she walked into the steaming bath water. She sat back and rested both hands on her stomach.

61

"Little unknown one, I have to get rid of you. You will always be in my heart. But after tomorrow, I will no longer remember you the way my mother forgot about me. It will cost you less pain in the long run! Too bad, I can't say the same about my pain. So, that is why I am sending you back where you belong. I know God understands! I am not ready for you right now, and I will not abandon you the way my mother abandoned me. To tell you the truth, little unknown one, I would rather my mom and dad done the same thing to me. If they have of, I would not be pregnant right now by a rapist with you. And how would you turn out? Probably not good!" Evie reached forward and turned off the water.

"I think God will understand." Evie spoke to herself and broke down.

"He knows the humiliation I am going through. I would not be a good mother right now to you. I wouldn't know where to start! Even if I did have you, I would probably end up murdering you anyway, if I didn't kill myself first! So, I'd rather get rid of you while you're unable to feel it." Evie scooted down in the tub. She closed her eyes and took deep breaths, as tears dropped down her face.

"This could've been avoided if only my father had listened to you mom! Daddy, I don't believe you cheated on us! Is that the reason why you never took her to pick up Justin? You were too concerned about Keisha finding out about my mother. Now look – It's costing me my entire life because of your disobedience. But what difference does this make? After tomorrow, God is probably through with me." Evie vented, as she slapped the bath water in anger.

Chapter Seven
Blindly Confused

The next day, Mrs. Thompson sat at her desk while she waited for her students to enter the classroom, specifically Evie. Her anticipation was to apologize to Evie, she waited patiently for her arrival.

"Something's not right!" Mrs. Thompson thought to herself as she analyzed Evie's story. "My honor student comes to class with a black eye?" She shook her head in disbelief as Mrs. Thompson watched students enter her classroom, walking to their desk. Mrs. Thompson stood up from behind her desk, while resting both hands on the arms. With a strut to the board, she erased yesterday's assignment, and then she turned around towards the class. The bell rang.

"Good morning class!" Mrs. Thompson greeted. Her class responded as her eyes roamed at Evie's empty desk. Little did she know Evie was lying on a surgical table, almost unconscious, soon to be rid of a life that she did not ask for.

◆◆◆◆◆

The doctor entered. "Miss Young? Miss Young? Can you hear me?" Evie is silenced on the white clothed table. The doctor began the abortion procedure as the nurse assisted. Through the machine the baby's heartbeat vanished.

Hours later, Evie exited the abortion clinic. They rolled her into the waiting area in a wheelchair. Another nurse came minutes later, to give her a prescription along with instructions.

"Miss Young, you must take these twice a day with food. Do you

need us to call you an Uber?" Evie looked at the nurse with both eyes widen, with a red ring around the unswollen one.

"That will be fine." Evie agreed. "And thank you all for taking care of me." The nurse smiled at Evie's statement, and then gave her a clipboard with papers to sign.

"Thank you!" Evie returned the clipboard to the nurse. The nurse laid the clipboard on the counter, and she rolled Evie through the front door. An Uber pulled in front of them. An Ethiopian man hopped out helping the nurse to get Evie into the back seat of the vehicle.

"Thank you." Evie smiled as the driver closed the door and waved back at the nurse. The Ethiopian man got in and drove off. She relaxed her neck on the back of the headrest, humming a song her mother sang to her the night before she disappeared.

Tears dripped. Evie swallowed her pain and sorrow. The Uber driver glanced at Evie through the rearview mirror. Before she knew it, they've arrived back at her motel. He pulled up to the front door, and then got out to open the door for Evie.

"Thank you, sir." The Ethiopian driver smiled at Evie's appreciative words.

"You're quite welcome ma'am. You have a bless day." Mrs. Klein spotted Evie and walked out to the Uber.

"Are you okay? Can you make it?" Mrs. Klein walked towards Evie. "I will take her from here." Mrs. Klein responded and tipped the driver $50 in his hand.

The man looked in his hand and his face lite up. "God bless you! Thank you." The driver got into the vehicle and drove out of sight. Mrs. Klein walked Evie to her room door. Evie took out her keycard from her shoulder purse. She attempted to open the door, but she paused.

"Why are you being so nice to me?" Evie looked at Mrs. Klein.

"You don't trust anyone." Mrs. Klein discerned in her spirit. "God has sent me to help you get on the right track with Him. The enemy has a trap to kill and destroy your life just like he does my daughter." Evie looked at her strangely.

"I know this may sound strange to you, but God has anointed me to pray for people who are under demonic attacks." Evie remained silent while they proceeded toward her room. Upon opening the door Evie found beautiful flowers of every kind, balloons, gifts, homemade food, and deserts. Evie walked in rather astonished.

"How did you know I was coming back?" Evie questioned Mrs. Klein with a smile.

"Well...." Mrs. Klein made a slight hand gesture. "You didn't return the key and I saw that you didn't check out in the computer."

"Duh!" Evie responded with a smile. Mrs. Klein closed the front door while Evie walked closer to the food. Mrs. Klein stepped forward and rests her hands at her waistline.

"Give God all the praise Evie. He's the one who instructed me to arrange all of this for you." Evie is mesmerized by all of the gifts in her room. She began to shed tears. Evie sat at the foot of the bed dropping her head down. Mrs. Klein gently walked over to

Evie and sat close beside her. She opened her arms and drew Evie into them. Both ladies hugged.

"I don't deserve any of this!" Evie spoke "How can you say that the Lord sent you, when I am a mess?" Evie questioned Mrs. Klein. Evie's purse fell off her shoulder. Mrs. Klein took a deep breath and embraced Evie with comfort. She pulled her close, as a mother does her child.

"What I would like for you to do beautiful, is change into these clean pajamas that the Lord has blessed you with, then I would like for you to eat something and rest." Mrs. Klein spoke softly to Evie.

"God placed all of this on my heart to do just for you. So, rest in Him! He has seen what you've endured the past eight years." Strangely, Evie looked up to Mrs. Klein's statement.

"What did you say?" Evie questioned her comment.

"I said God have seen everything you've endured these past eight years. I am just one of His messengers Evie. He sent me to help you." Mrs. Klein looked at Evie while she stood up. Quickly she slipped her feet out of her mule sneakers, grabbed her new pair of white silk pajamas from the burgundy chair, and then walked into the bathroom. Evie closed the door behind her.

"Who is this lady?" Evie talked to herself in the mirror. "She really doesn't know what I've been through." Evie slipped down her pants with shame and ignored the reflection of herself in the mirror. The aroma of food came from underneath the door. Evie folded her clothes up, placing them in her hand. She opened the door and threw them in the corner. Evie walked to the queen-size bed. Mrs. Klein turned around and walked away from the window

towards Evie. "Evie why don't you lie down, and I'll get you some food." Mrs. walked to the left side of Evie's bed and pulled out a bed tray. She placed the plate of food on her tray and served Evie.

"Go ahead and chow down!" Evie looked at the food. All of a sudden, her attitude changed.

"Don't eat that, she probably poisoned it. You don't know that lady. She could be a friend of your Aunt Tammy." An evil deceiving voice spoke to Evie.

"Yeah! She's not sent from God. Just think about it, Evie. Your aunt and uncle are trying to set you up and kill you." The evil voice continued to speak.

In rage, Evie jumped up and threw the table of food to the side.

"Who are you?" Evie demanded with anger in her eyes. "You're trying to flatter me with gifts and food, and then set me up to be killed." Evie perceived and stood.

"I will not fall into their crazy trap." Evie pointed her finger while she stood in a defensive position.

The Spirit of God fell heavily upon Mrs. Klein, **"I have given you dominion over the earth. I have granted you power to cast out demons, to tread upon scorpions. Now take authority – NOW."** The Spirit of God spoke. Suddenly Mrs. Klein's voice tone changed.

"In the name of Jesus!" Mrs. Klein boldly spoke. Evie stared at her suitcase.

"Shoot her!" The evil voice demanded Evie. Evie walked towards her suitcase, opened it, and pulled out the chrome 45-caliber gun to Mrs. Klein's forehead.

"In the authoritative name of Jesus, I speak to you Satan..." Mrs. Klein pointed to Evie as the gun was to her head.

"I command every unclean spirit to come out of Evie Young in the name of Jesus." Evie began to breakdown and wiped her eyes. Mrs. Klein prayed in tongues. Evie began to shake, and then she dropped the gun. Mrs. Klein continued praying in tongues as she quickly looked around for a towel. She picked up the gun with it and placed it on the lower shelf of the TV stand. Evie gagged, spitting up vomit on the carpet. Mrs. Klein reached over Evie grabbing the black trashcan. Mrs. Klein placed it in front of Evie.

"No! No!" Evie screamed, wrapping her hands around her neck. Evie chocked herself. Her face turned red. Mrs. Klein grabbed Evie's hands from around her neck.

"Loose your stronghold off of Evie... you suicide spirit. I bind you up in the name of Jesus and I send you into a dry desolate place in the name of Jesus and I command you to never return. Spirit of fear, I cast you out, in the name of Jesus. Every foul and demonic force that has been operating in Evie's life, I command you to come out right now, in the name of Jesus. And I loose peace upon Evie, the Spirit of the Living God, and His purpose for her life to rest upon her, in the name of Jesus." Evie wept. She remained on the floor over the trashcan, on her knees.

"Help Evie to the bed and speak My word to her." The Spirit of God spoke.

Mrs. Klein placed both her arms under Evie's. "Let's walk over to

the bed." Mrs. Klein suggested. Slowly Evie relaxed herself in the bed. Mrs. Klein walked into the bathroom to get some tissues, as Evie snuggled herself under her covers. Mrs. Klein walked over to Evie's bed and handed her the tissue while sitting down next to Evie.

"God knows what you have done today, Evie. He is very much against what has happened. However, you never had anyone to teach you. God forgives you and He gives mercy to those who lack knowledge. Evie, God's desire is for you to know Him. He wants you to seek Him and submit to His will for your life. He wants to teach you his voice, so that He can order your footsteps." Mrs. Klein stared into Evie's eyes. Evie sat up straight in the bed listening intently.

"God has seen all you have been through as a young child. He is not holding you accountable for the filthiness your young body experienced. But He is calling you into repentance. I am going to show you according to God's word how He expects us to live. You are special to Him, but demonic forces have been assigned to destroy you."

"Who are you, a fortune-teller? Everything that you're saying is true!" Evie questioned.

"No, I am not a fortune-teller. God is the only one that sees and knows everything. So, the Spirit of God manifest itself through one of His vessels, giving them the power and insight. He revealed these things concerning you." Mrs. Klein stared at Evie, and then the Voice of God intervenes.

"Evie was taught my Word as a young girl, but she was left by the wayside. She must learn and live by My Word, and when she does the forces of darkness will not prevail against her.

Share with Evie the story of Daniel." The Spirit of God instructed Mrs. Klein. She goes into the story of Daniel as Evie looked at her attentively.

"Daniel was a Prophet of God who was sent to a king named Nebuchadnezzar to give him several messages [Daniel Chapter 2]. But there's one message I would like to point out to you. Nebuchadnezzar was the king of Babylon in Daniel's time. Verses two through four explain how the king had a dream one particular night that disturbed him. He called all the astrologers, magicians, enchanters, and sorcerers and demanded them to come to him. So, the king tells all of these magicians, astrologers, enchanters, and sorcerers to interpret the dream in which he had. And, they all said to the king, 'Tell us the dream, and I will tell you what it meant.' So, they went back and forth. Basically, they could not tell King Nebuchadnezzar the meaning of the dream, unless he gave them the dream first. Now remember Evie, I don't know anything about you, nor did you tell me anything." Mrs. Klein explained as she continued.

"In verse 24, Daniel, the prophet of God, was able to interpret the dream. So let me explain to you what a prophet is. They are specifically God's messengers, through whom God speaks divinely. God reveals to them information regarding His 'Divine Will' for a person's life. In addition, if he or she is out of the will of God, evil and danger surrounds them continually. God will either speak a word of warning before destruction, or blessings into his or her life.

A prophet also reveals things that will happen to people if they do not turn from their wicked ways. Destruction will come upon them. So, when a prophet stands before you Evie, be aware of God loving you so much, that He sent you His messengers to help warn, lead and guide you." Mrs. Klein stood up and walked to the window. Evie listened. "One thing about God's protection Evie, He will protect us from danger, and all evil and harm that try to come

70

our way. But it's only through the obedience of God's word that permits Him to protect us fully. The only way the enemy has free-range to attack our lives is through two things. First, he takes advantage of our vulnerability due to our lack of knowledge concerning the word of God." Evie continued to stare at Mrs. Klein while she explained.

"The second thing is, he manipulates those who know the Word but refuse to listen to the truth because of their disobedience." Mrs. Klein does an about face and walked back from the window toward Evie and picked the tray up from the floor.

"For example, my daughter is twenty. She has rejected the word of God. Her Father is a true and faithful Bishop. But our daughter, refused to listen. She runs the streets, using her body in every unclean way that you can imagine. I am aware of these things by the Spirit of God. The Bible instructs children to obey their parents and that is something she refuses to do. The spirit of disobedience rules her life." Mrs. Klein continued to share.

"My husband and I have done our jobs." Mrs. Klein placed the tray on the table. She walked over to the black trash can where Evie had vomited and tied a knot into the white bag.

"The only thing the Bishop and I can do now is pray for her and know that God will take care of the situation. Our only prayer is that she comes into repentance and give her life completely over to the Lord. We can't do that part for her, that a choice only she can make. " Evie stared at Mrs. Klein upon her last statement.

"So, what do you do if you had parents up until you were eight, then all of a sudden they disappear one day?" Evie paused in thought before she continued.

"My experience in life has taken me through so much harm and evil. I never had anyone to teach me, protect me or guide me. So how would I know how to live a life that pleases God?"

"The first step is to repent!" Mrs. Klein boldly stated as she looked into Evie's eyes. She continued to pick up the mess from the floor.

"God does not hold you accountable for the things you do not know." Mrs. Klein looked at Evie. Mrs. Klein placed the plastic cup into the trashcan, and then walked over to Evie. She held her hand.

"Evie baby, look at me... the Spirit of the Lord allowed me to give you that story for the benefit of this message. I am a prophet who is sent divinely from God. He has ordered my footsteps to help you." Mrs. Klein replied as she bent down and reached into her purse. She took out a black, leather journal and opened it to a page.

"I was in prayer all day yesterday and early this morning for you. My heart was very, very heavy Evie. I just couldn't shake you off. So, I began to pray in the spirit..." Evie interrupted.

"By the way, what was that language you were speaking?" Evie questioned.

"It's a spiritual gift God gives to His people, it's called being filled with the Holy Ghost, with the evidence of speaking in tongues." Mrs. Klein smiled at Evie before she continued.

"Speaking in tongues is the most intelligent and perfect language in the universe. The Holy Spirit bare witness through your heavenly language that authorizes you to communicate directly into The Spirit of God." Mrs. Klein cracked a smile at Evie.

"You are a spirit being first Evie, before you were made flesh. You are perfectly made in God's image. Only the Spirit of God is perfect. He perfects us. When we don't allow the spirit of The Living God to live within us, demonic forces can easily take residence on the inside of us instead. God's Spirit within us wants to dwell, live, move, and have its very being. And above all, the good spirit of God, wants to teach us how to listen and detect His good voice, from the evil voice, and your own voice. I know that some bad things have happened to you because God's voice was ignored."

Evie interrupted her. "What bad stuff are you referring to?" Evie questioned. Mrs. Klein sighed.

"In prayer Evie, God revealed to me some things. He showed me a vision of a herd of sheep. One particular sheep was in a fence near two shepherds, and then they ended up leaving the sheep unattended. So, the sheep ended up being placed under the care of another shepherd. But this shepherd was a wolf in disguise. Once the disguised shepherd received the sheep in its herd he chased them down, trying to kill them. But the sheep did not get killed. However, it became dreadfully wounded as it laid in the herd with blood pouring out onto the ground, crying out for help. God sent an angel to rescue the sheep and the sheep never saw that shepherd again. When I met you the other day and saw your black eye, compassion filled my heart. God led me to pray for you. In my spirit, I knew some things weren't right." Mrs. Klein turned the page in her book.

"I don't understand. What does that story have to do with me?" Evie lifted her back off a propped pillow upon her question.

"The sheep represents you Evie, being unprotected. Your parents walked away from you and have never come back. The enemy has attacked them and is working his way towards killing you. So, you

followed after another shepherd, thinking they were going to take care of you. But, once you got there, they turned into wolves, wounding you. A shepherd basically represents someone guarding and protecting over you." Mrs. Klein crossed her legs and made gestures with her right hand.

"After your parents didn't return, you had to live amongst wolves. They weren't any good for you. They pretended to be! Once they got you, you were…" Mrs. Klein wept, finishing her thought.

"You were touched in all the wrong ways!" Mrs. Klein went on to explain.

"No one paid attention to you correctly. After your parents disappeared, you stopped being taught the word of God. The wolves managed to chase you down. One of them caught you and began digging into you until bloodshed. The blood poured out to the ground. That represents being raped." Mrs. Klein painfully revealed the vision. Evie looked up at her astonished. She turned red, then burst into tears. Mrs. Klein cried with Evie, hugging her.

"Once your relative raped you he continued to do so for the entire time you were in his herd. In this case, the herd represents his territory, similar to Egypt. When you read in the Old Testament about the Israelites being in Egypt, they were slaves under King Pharaoh. There was no escape until God sent a man named Moses to help lead them out of slavery. You were a slave to your uncle Evie. God sent an angel to instruct you to get away before he killed you! Your heart has been crying out for help. God heard you! And your parents have not been found nor have they found you." Mrs. Klein looked at Evie, flustered in tears. Evie continued to break down while shaking her head back and forth.

"God has heard my prayers. He is the one who has directed you to me." Evie agreed wiping away snot from her nose with a balled-up

piece of white bathroom tissue. An angel came into my room and warned me, if I didn't leave that house, I was going to die the next day!" Mrs. Klein looked at Evie as she spoke.

"Is that where your black eye came from?" Evie shook her head to confirm. Mrs. Klein grabbed Evie and hugged her tightly. The Spirit of the Lord revealed a vision of a large tree bearing fruit. Suddenly the fruit fell off the branches, smashing to the ground being destroyed. Mrs. Klein looked at Evie.

"Were you pregnant? Evie looked down in shame, nodding her head with tears rushing down her face.

"I'm a murderer! God will never forgive me for what I have done!" Evie cried out. Mrs. Klein lifted Evie's chin and looked squarely into her eyes.

"God is against abortion Evie. He is the only one who gives life. Women who carry babies are only the bearers. God breathes the breath of life in our blood. And He grants breath in the baby when it is conceived. In the bible there are numerous scriptures that speak about taking one's life, [Exodus 20:13 NKJ] is one of them." Mrs. Klein picked up her bible and turn to the scripture.

"Do not murder," which is one of the Ten Commandments. But when you lack knowledge of God's word, His mercy and grace cover you. So, I am not condemning you and neither is God!" Mrs. Klein turned the pages to another scripture then hands the Bible to Evie.

"Here read this, John 3:17 [NKJ]." Mrs. Klein pointed to the scripture. Evie took the bible. "For God did not send His son into the world to condemn the world, but that the world through Him might be saved." Evie reads with the Bible laid across her lap, she

75

stretched out her legs. "Jesus's blood has paid the price for you Evie. The scripture says in Psalms 139:13 [NKJ]." Mrs. Klein shared.

"For You did form my inward parts; You knit me together in my mother's womb." Mrs. Klein quoted.

"Evie, abortions are wrong. It's God who creates and knit us together in our mother's womb and gives life." Mrs. Klein looked at Evie with a serious look.

"You must make a huge decision and submit yourself to God Evie, this day forward. Then, you need a church home, so you are taught the word of God properly, grow spiritually and have an under shepherd who can help watch over your soul. An under shepherd is a Pastor." Mrs. Klein specified.

"You must Evie, if not death is on its way, slowly but surely to destroy you. So let me prophesy to you again." Mrs. Klein reiterated.

"You must answer God's calling now, and if you refuse Him, He cannot protect you the way He would like. Death will surely follow you. The information I gave you the other day, is about our church. We would love to have you." Mrs. Klein smiled at Evie and gave her a hug.

"I have a question for you." Mrs. Klein questioned, placing her hands together and folded them while looking at Evie.

"Do you believe that God formed His Spirit into flesh and came to earth through Christ?" Mrs. Klein asked.

"Yes, I believe."

"Have you confessed Romans 10:9 and 10:10 out loud?" Mrs. Klein asked.

"I don't remember. I was baptized when I was seven."

"Baptism alone doesn't save you." Mrs. Klein explained Corinthians 5:17 [NKJ].

"Therefore, if anyone is in Christ Jesus, he is a new creation; old things have passed away; behold, all things have become new."

"Baptism is a symbol of you living a new life and becoming a new creature in Christ Jesus. Basically, you're telling the Lord once you go down in the water you are killing your old ways. When you come up, you are a new creature who's going to live a holy life, set apart from the world, through the renewing of your mind. When you get a chance read Romans chapter 12, verse 2. So, if you have never confessed Jesus as your Lord and Savior, allowing Him to come into your heart, you are not saved. If you are a devil before you go down in the water, you'll come up as a wet one. It doesn't matter if you were brought up in a church or have backslid. We can take care of that right now. I would like you to pray these words with me." Mrs. Klein encouraged Evie to repeat after her. She extended her hands out to Evie. They both held hands while closing their eyes. Mrs. Klein prayed.

"Dear Lord, come into my life in the name of Jesus and save me now. Lord I believe in Jesus Christ, and I believe He shed His blood for all my sins. He died and rose from the dead and is alive right now! Lord, I also repent of all my sins and shortcomings and turn away from them right now. In Jesus' name I thank you Lord for rebirthing me and making me yours again in Jesus' name, Amen!"

"Amen!" Evie repeated, hugging Mrs. Klein. Slowly Mrs. Klein walked around the room, and then stopped and looked at Evie.

"There is one other thing I would like to point out to you in the book of Mark, and oh yeah, I have this Bible for you." Mrs. Klein handed Evie a bible.

"When you get a chance, I would like you to read Mark, Chapter 4, Verses 1-20 as well. It teaches what happens when the word goes forth. In Verse 15, it teaches how Satan comes immediately to take whatever word that has been sown into your heart. And in your case, it's your salvation that he wants." Mrs. Klein paused in empathy.

"This is why so many people backslide. They don't know that they have an evil, who walks back in forth seeking whom he may devour; 1Peter 5:8. In the scripture is says, 'Be sober,' why; because Satan will use any and everything, to pull you back into the old you, before you can realize it. So, if you are not watchful or don't have someone to help watch over your soul, Satan will overtake you." Mrs. Klein walked over to her purse. She picked it up and placed it on her shoulder. Evie sat up and stood her feet.

"Just for comfort, I have not always been saved Evie, and I also had an abortion at the age of sixteen. No one taught me the word of God or how to resist evil. I began to study the word for myself. If you can read Matthew, Mark, Luke and John, those books will teach you on how to live, walk and operate in this earthly body. Christ was our prime example." Mrs. Klein continued.

"There is no good thing in our flesh according to Romans 7:18. It will always lead you wrong. But if you keep in mind that God has called you from your mother's womb. He already knew your name. Without God, we are nothing and we'll never find our way without the good Spirit' guidance."

Both ladies smiled at her other and hugged. "You get some rest. When I get home, I am going to talk to my husband to see how we can help you get out of this motel. You're only 16, and in what, the eleventh grade?" Mrs. Klein guessed as Evie nodded.

"Do you have an absent note for today?" Mrs. Klein inquired.

"I forgot to ask for one." Evie replied.

"What school do you attend?"

"Wilson High School on Cedar Courts." Evie answered.

"I know exactly where that is. I am going to your school so they can excuse you for today. I'll personally go to the clinic to pick an excused notice. Just give me the name of the abortion center, and I'll pick it up for you. Just call them and let them know your mom is on her way." Evie looked at Mrs. Klein strangely upon her statement.

"Consider me as your spiritual mother. It's not a lie." Mrs. Klein stated. Evie smiled at just the thought of Mrs. Klein's idea.

"Thank you so much!" Evie replied.

"Rest your body so it can heal. I will call your room later or come by to check on you!" Mrs. Klein reassured Evie as she walked toward the front door. Evie followed behind her.

"I would like to see you stable and finish high school. And whatever we can do to help you, my husband and I will." Evie smiled. "I appreciate all you have done Mrs. Klein." Evie

expressed gratitude. Mrs. Klein kissed Evie on her forehead, which brought back memories when Evie's dad kissed her on the forehead. "Call me if you need me." Mrs. Klein smiled.

"I'll call you later, after I speak to Bishop Klein. Go get some rest! Don't worry about the crumbs on the floor. When I go on shift tonight, I'll make sure it's cleaned up." Mrs. Klein grinned exit, until she remembered.

"Oh, I almost forgot that we need to get rid of this!" Mrs. Klein walked over to the gun, wrapped it in the white towel and placed it in her purse.

"I'm going to pray that God leads me to where I need to dispose this. My protecting angels will make sure no one finds it."

"Are you sure?" Evie questioned.

"Trust God!" Mrs. Klein confidently spoke walking toward the door and gracefully exiting. Evie grabbed the doorknob and closed the door, locking it. Evie walked back toward the bed and the evil voice does exactly what the bible spoke about in Mark 4.

"See you trust everybody. How do you know this lady is not setting you up to kill you? If I were you, I would stay by myself. You know she was just trying to be nice to trap you and kill you. I bet she's going to try and kill you when you're sleeping. That's why she took the gun." The voice continued filling Evie's head with fear and lies. The deceptive spirit continued.

"Why don't you just go ahead and leave, so when she gets back, she won't find you! You don't need anyone but yourself. You have money and if you run out just go and sell yourself. You saw what type of money you made over the years. You don't need anyone

to help you. You can buy your own apartment. If you go with her, she is going to turn you into a religious nun and control you." Evie vulnerably continued to entertain the thoughts of the evil voice.

"Yeah, before you know it, you'll be 17, then 18; you won't need anyone to show you anything. You can have everything you ever wanted. You don't need parents. The only thing you need is money. It's better than anything. Now leave! Leave before she comes back and hurt you. Look at your granny, she's a pastor's wife and look how wicked she is." The voices rants on. Evie is confused.

"I am tired of running and going through this drama." Evie yelled while slapping her right-hand on the mattress.

"And on the other hand, how do I know that Mrs. Klein isn't after me? No one else ever believed me. What makes me think she really believes me anyway? Why should I trust her word?" Evie questioned as she ran her hands through her curly hair.

"You know what? I just want to be alone. I don't want to be bothered with anyone!" Evie insisted as she pulled down her pajama pants and threw them across the room. Then she took off her pajama top, tossing it on the bed. Evie walked to the corner by the bathroom, picking up her folded clothes. She walked back to the bed when the phone rang.

Evie paused and stared at the ringing phone while she rushed to put on her denim jeans and white shirt. The phone stopped ringing. She slipped her feet into her white mules that are located under the foot of her bed. Evie walked toward the front door pulling her roller suitcase alongside and exited. The door shut closed, Evie spotted a taxi driving by, she flagged them down. The driver stopped and popped open the trunk. The taxi driver gets

81

out and placed Evie's luggage in the trunk. Evie hopped inside the cab. The driver got in, closed the door, and drove off.

"Do you mind driving me to the front office? I need to check out." Evie asked. "Certainly. The cab driver pulled in front of the motel's lobby. Confused and blinded, Evie walked away from God's divine help.

◆◆◆◆◆

Mrs. Klein disposed the gun into a nearby river, getting back into her vehicle, she drove to the clinic. The Spirit of God alarmed and spoke.

"Pick up the phone and call Evie's room." The Spirit of the Lord commanded. Mrs. Klein dialed the number to the motel.

"Yes, Evie Young room please." Mrs. Klein requested the receptionist. The phone rang and rang but no answer. Mrs. Klein hung up. Placing her cell phone in the passenger seat, she sighed.

"Maybe she's asleep." Mrs. Klein assumed.
"She is not sleeping. Pray fervently." The Spirit of the God alarmed Mrs. Klein.

"When you return, you will find that she's gone. Your prayers will keep Evie." The Spirit of God spoke. Mrs. Klein u-turned her vehicle and headed back toward the motel. The cab passed by with Evie in it, unaware. Mrs. Klein reached the motel and pulled up in front of Evie's room. She quickly grabbed her purse and placed it on her left shoulder. She hopped out of her car and knocked on the door. Mrs. Klein knocked harder. No answer.

"Peek through the window." The Spirit of God spoke. Mrs. Klein walked away from the door. She slightly turned around and

82

peeked through a small opening. There's no Evie anywhere. Mrs. Klein dug inside her purse and grabbed her cell phone. She dials Evie's room.

"Room 173 please." Mrs. Klein looked inside the window again, looking puzzled. "She checked out?! When? Wow! Okay, thank you." Mrs. Klein hung up and slowly walked back to her car.

"You have done your job. The rest is up to Evie." The Spirit of the God reinsured. Mrs. Klein got in and drove to the front office of the motel. She stepped out and walked to the office door.

"Hello, Mrs. Klein!" The owner greeted her in an Arabic accent.

"Hello, Mr. Ashua!"

"You're early but I'm happy you're here! I'm afraid I have some bad news to share with you. Mrs. Ashua and I have decided that she will not go back to our country. So, she's going to help me out here. I'm afraid I'm not going to need your help any longer." Mrs. Klein looked at him. He continued.

"You are an excellent worker, and because of that I am going to give you your check today instead of Friday with a $300.00 bonus. I know I've scheduled you for tonight, but we've been slow, so I won't need you."

"Well, thank you!" Mrs. Klein expressed her appreciation by shaking his hand with a smile.

"God is good!" Mr. Ashua smiled Mrs. Klein's statement. "I know everything has a time, a place and a season. And God's work is

completed here!" She smiled as Mr. Ashua handed her the last paycheck.

"Thank you!" Mrs. Klein accepted it with joy.

"I'm sorry Mrs. Klein!" Mr. Ashua continued to apologize.

"There's no need for an apology Mr. Ashua. You have a blessed day!" Mrs. Klein turned around with a slight smile, and then walked toward the exit.

"You can drop by anytime!" Mr. Ashua insisted. Mrs. Klein grinned and walked out the door filled happiness. Evie remained on her mind. "You are in control!" Looking up towards the sky, Mrs. Klein smiled and got back into her vehicle and drove away.

Chapter Eight
The Mouth of Hell

The Bible teaches in Matthew 12:43-45, "When an unclean spirit goes out of a man he goes through dry places, seeking rest, and finds none. Then he says, I will return to my house from which I came. And when he comes, he finds it empty, swept and put in order. Then he goes and takes with him seven other spirits more wicked than himself, and they enter and dwell there, and the last state of that man is worse than the first. So shall it also be with this wicked generation."

Once, Evie accepted Christ in the motel room with Mrs. Klein, unclean spirits were cast out. Evie's job was to now work out her salvation, but instead she fell into the devil's trap that caused seven other unclean spirits more wicked than the first ones. Evie ended up in a worse state than before.

◆◆◆◆◆

"Thank you!" Evie grabbed her luggage from the cab driver. He got back into the cab, and then drove off. Evie looked around. She spotted the Savannah Mall and headed toward one of its nearby hotels.

"Whoa!" Evie became dizzy and light-headed, staggering toward a parking meter. She embraced it for support.

"I guess my pain meds are wearing off." Evie spoke out loud, as she held her head high walking into the hotel lobby. Evie stepped onto the elegant beige-marbled floors and goes straight to the reservation counter. Letting go of the handle of her luggage, she placed her backpack on the floor and her purse on the counter.

"Yes, how may I help you?" A Caucasian woman with blonde hair

greeted Evie. "I would like a room," Evie replied.

"A single bed or a double?"

"It doesn't matter! Whichever one you have available is fine!" Evie replied.

" For how long ma'am?"

"A week." Evie responded as she spotted a tall brown complexioned male smiling and staring her up and down.

"Okay ma'am from today through next Tuesday your balance is $1,200, not including tax." The front desk clerk informed.

"Okay, that's fine." Evie dug into her wallet.

"Can I see your ID please?" The blonde-haired lady stared at Evie, as she handed over her permit. The lady looked at it, and then handed it back to Evie.

"I'm sorry you're not 18 yet. I'm afraid I can't . . ."

Before the blonde finished her sentence, Evie laid out a stack of $100 on the counter. "Here, I am a customer! Please lady, I need a room. So, as you were saying . . ." Evie sarcastically reiterated her request, gathering the money and handing it to her.

The clerk took the money swiftly out of Evie's hand and smiled. She then placed the money on the lower counter in front of her, as she began to type in some numbers.

"With tax, your total is $1,225. Normally, we only accept credit cards. But I will make an exception for you today." Evie handed over an extra $20. The woman retrieved it, and then printed out a receipt, placing it in Evie's hand. Evie smiled when the lady gave her the keycard.

"Your room number is 115. It's straight down the hall and on your right." Evie bended to get her backpack and placed it on her left shoulder. She gathered her suitcase, stepped onto the marble floor, and headed towards her room.

"115..." Evie walked past rooms, looking for hers. Stopping at the cherry wood door, she placed the keycard in, and then pushed the door open. Evie rolled her suitcase inside the room. She stepped onto the cushioned-carpet, turned on the lights and sniffed the fresh-powdered aroma that greets her. She stood still for a moment, admiring the room' ambiance. "Oh wow! This is amazing!" The backpack fell from her shoulder, onto the floor. Evie laid across the bed in exhaustion, she curled up, wrapped herself with the comforter and drifted to sleep.

◆◆◆◆◆

Hours later, Evie's empty stomach woke her up. Her hunger led her out of her room and into the Savannah Mall. She walked past several people and stores as she headed toward the food court. Evie stopped to look at a fashionable outfit displayed on a Caucasian mannequin located in a store window. She admired the low-cut, backless cream shirt, on display with a pair of dark brown denim pants.

"I wish I could have that... man I am running out of cash quick." Evie looked into her purse, counting the bills in her wallet. She sighed.

"What are you going to do now Evie?" A voice spoke within. Evie

shook off the temptation and walked away. "I wonder how much this outfit costs?" Evie inquired as the oldie's music filled the air. She returned back to the window display, viewing the clothing. Evie looked at the price tag.

"$250.00 . . . man?!" Evie shouted out loud.

"I got to have it!" Evie openly debated with herself, not realizing that a nearby by-stander was observing.

"You can have it!" The 5'6, brown-complexioned young lady replied. Evie turned around and stared.

"Excuse me?" Evie looked at the young lady for an explanation.

"I said you can have it!" The strange young lady reinsured.

"Okay...how do you figure?" With a chuckle, Evie waited for her response.

"With this!" The strange young lady slid her right-hand inside her front baggy jean pocket and pulled out a bundle of $100 bills. She took off the silver clip, unfolded them and counted them. Evie's eyes widen, staring at the money, and then the strange young lady.

"What size do you wear?" She touched the outfits Evie was staring at. The strange young lady looked through the rack of clothes for Evie's size. Evie stared off in a daze.

"Is this a blessing from God?" Evie questioned within herself.

"**It's a trap!**" The Spirit of God spoke within Evie. "**Don't be**

deceived by what you see. I'm the only One who can supply your every need."** The Spirit of God reinforced.

"You are in need, and besides God wants you to have the best, so take it!" Another voice spoke within Evie. She shook her head back and forth, battling with the conflicting voices.

"So, is that a, yes? " The strange young lady waited for Evie's response, who stood in a daze, battling with the voices.

"Seek after the Lord your God and all these things shall be added to you." The Spirit of God spoke.

"Hello! Sure, take your time! We got until the sun goes down. Psss...maybe you do. I don't!" The young lady sarcastically spoke.

"Take it, take it!" An inner voice spoke persistently. Evie stared in battled. The strange lady put her money back inside her pocket and walked away.

"You're stupid! You need money. You are running out of money. Those $100 bills can be yours!" Evie watched the stranger strut away from her towards the front of the department store, as her intuition spoke.

"Wait!" Evie walked towards her. The strange young lady stopped and turned around with a smirk that highlighted her dimples. She licked her dark brown lips, walking toward Evie. They meet halfway. Evie swallowed her pride with an exhale.

"Hi...I'm Evie." She extended her right hand out.

"Sheila!" With a smile, she shook Evie's hand.

"Evie is a nice name." Evie blushed at her compliment.

"So, I'm assuming you changed your mind?" Shelia looked at Evie for an explanation.

"Actually, one of my reasons for being in the Mall was to fill out job applications." Evie's transparency caught Sheila's attention, who resumed to looking for Evie's size. Sheila's eyes roam back at Evie.

"What's your size again baby girl!"

"A six." Evie revealed.

"Bang! There it is!" Sheila pulled out Evie's size, holding the outfit up against her. Evie looked at herself in the long mirror, both ladies smiled, and then head toward the checkout counter.

"You said that you were looking for a job?" Sheila reiterated.

"I got you on that too!" Evie looked at her. "For real?!" Evie smiled.

"For real!" Sheila smiled back. "I got you ma! Pick out whatever else you want. It's on me! If you don't see something in this store, you got the entire mall to choose from."

"Oh wow! I don't know what to say." Evie's face lit up with a smile, looking at the belts on the rack. "Thank you, Sheila!"

"Get that beige one, that'll look great on you." Sheila smiled.

"You think so?" Evie questioned.

"Yeah! The red one too." Sheila suggested.

"Okay!" Evie grabbed it, while picking out two other outfits. Both ladies walked to the register. Sheila continued to pick out different outfits she thought Evie would look good in. Evie walked ahead of her, picking out a short red skirt.

"Here this should fit you, what do you think?" Sheila walked over to Evie for her opinion. "That's pretty too!" Evie agreed.

"Here this is for you too." Sheila looked at Evie, who slightly smiled with suspense.

"Why are you being so nice? And... when do I have to pay you back?" Evie questioned Sheila.

"That's my nature and there are no strings attached. All of this is on me. Count it as a blessing in disguise." Shelia replied.

"I'm just blessed Evie and felt like you had a need." Sheila expressed to Evie who gave the clothes to the cashier. As the items rang up, the cashier glanced at Evie with a grin, while Sheila took out the stack of money.

"Your total is $1780.72." Sheila counted $1800.00, handed it to the cashier, clipped the remaining stack, and placed it back into her pocket. The cashier accepted the total, counted Shelia's change, and then closed the cash drawer. Grabbing the receipt,

the cashier handed Sheila her change. "Give it to her." Shelia instructed the cashier who handed the change to Evie. She took in by surprised.

"Thank you!" Sheila told the cashier, handing the shopping bag to Evie.

"Wow...thank you so much!" Evie spoke in gratitude, while they walked toward the exit.

"Let's go!" Sheila smiled.

"Have you eaten?" Shelia held the door, exiting the store.

"No, I haven't," Evie replied.

"What do you have a taste for?" Sheila inquired, both ladies walked the mall. "Whatever! It doesn't matter to me. I'm just hungry." Evie smiled at Sheila.

"Has my misery come to an end? I guess God has answered my prayers!" Evie thoughts spoke. Sheila walked alongside Evie, cool and nonchalant, balling her fist against her mouth and gazing at Evie from head to toe. They reached an exit that led them into the mall parking lot.

"You're my type of girl Evie." Sheila held the door and they exited towards Sheila's car. Evie became speechless questioning why the strange young lady is being so nice to her.

"I believe you would like Rays Classic." Sheila suggested.

"You'll like their food. Oh yeah, I'd like to introduce you to Tank and Tracey. Those are my business partners." Sheila chirped the alarm to her metallic convertible Mercedes CK 320. She unlocked the doors, Evie opened the door and stepped in.

"Alexa...call Tank." Shelia told Alexa to dial.

"Hello?"

"Tank, it's Sheila! Listen, can you and Tracey meet me at Rays Classic? I would like to introduce you to a beautiful young lady who is looking to make some money. Okay, see you in a minute." Sheila clicked on the phone icon on her steering wheel.

"Who are these guys you're introducing me to?"

"Tank and Tracey own several of businesses and I believe they will hire you on the spot. The cash you saw, you can make in one day." Sheila spoke in confidence while driving with her left-hand on the steering wheel and the other hand shifted gears.

"Do you have a car?"

"I don't." Evie looked at Shelia.

"We'll need to get you a car first. This type of job requires a lot of traveling." Sheila glanced at Evie, and then resumed her eyes back to the road.

"Hold up!" Evie looked at Sheila with a smile. Sheila turned into the parking lot of the restaurant, shifting gear into park.

"You're automatically assuming that I'm going to like this job you're offering?" Evie giggled in inquiry.

"Well, let me ask you, how soon do you need money?"

"Immediately!" Evie responded.

Sheila turned off the ignition, taking out the keys. "Trust me! Everyone we hire is well taken care of!" Sheila reassured.

"Well, I am telling you now, I'm not selling drugs! Evie boldly spoke.

"Relaxed! I'm not a drug dealer." Sheila slightly smiled, the two ladies got out of the car and walked into the restaurant. Sheila held the door for Evie. The server greeted.

"Table for two?" The host smiled.

"Actually, a table for four. We're expecting two other guests. Evie looked at Shelia upon her statement.

"Sure...follow me." Evie walked in front of Sheila, who studied Evie from behind. Shelia texted Tracey and Tank. The server sat Evie and Sheila near the Teddy White live band. Evie slid in on one side. Sheila followed. The melody of the bass guitarist stood out from the rest of the band. Evie stared at the energy the drummer released. He played. She closed her eyes and bopped her head to the rhythm. Sheila nudged; Evie eyes opened wide.

"Come on, we can order while we wait." Sheila gazed into the menu.

Sheila looked up to Tracey and Tank walking towards the table. Tracey glided down the aisle first, greeting another table first. Tank followed. "Hey ma!" Pearly white teeth, Tank smiled.

"How are you?" Sheila stood up to greet them, hugging Tank. Tracey moved toward Evie's side, looking at her with a smile. Sheila slid into the booth. Tank sat next to her.

"Tracey...Tank meet Evie." Sheila pointed. Evie grinned at them. "How you doing?" Tank extended his hand, Evie shook it. He licked his lips in a cool way.

"I'm Tracey." Evie stared at his lips in her face. "Didn't I see you today in the hotel lobby?" Evie looked into Tracey's eyes.

"Yep, that was me. I was checking your fine ass out!" Tracey flirtatious gestor made Evie blush. Evie inhaled as his cologne hypnotized her. She closed her eyes to hold in his sweet smell, and then exhaled hugging her close.

"This was meant to be!" Tracey whispered in Evie's ear. She smiled at him. Tank jealously looked at Tracey.

"Okay, can we eat now?" Sheila suggested. Tracey released Evie. Sheila looked at Evie and smiled. She talked to Tank looking back Evie's way.

"Talk to me baby!" Tracey looked at menu and resumed back to Evie while she looked into her menu.

"Sheila tells me that you are in need of a job!"

"Well, yes I am," Evie cleared her throat. "How old are you?" Tracey inquires. "I just turned seventeen." Everyone at the table focused their eyes on Evie.

The waitress walked over to the table. "Hi, my name is Kim, and I will be your server today. What can I get you all to drink?" Tracey looked at her with a smile. Kim smiled back.

"I'll have lemonade," Tracey ordered.

"I'll have an iced tea," Tank looked at Kim.

"I'll have water with lemons on the side." Sheila ordered.

"And, you can give me an iced tea and lemonade mixed, with two lemons please. Evie looked at Kim, while Tracey and Tank looked at each other. "Okay. Got it!" Kim wrote down everyone's drinks. "Are you guys ready to order?"

"I am." Sheila looked up and closed the menu. Evie put down her menu as well.

"I will have the Lobster tails with the super jumbo stuffed shrimps, and a basket of garlic cheese bread." Ordered Sheila.

"I will have a whole Lobster with the Shrimp Fettuccini and another order of garlic bread." Tank told Kim, she wrote down both orders, while looking at Tracey. "Are you ready sir?"

"I am going to let the lady go first." Tracey gazed at Evie with a smile.

"Man, all of your orders are intimidating compared to what I want." Evie looked across at Shelia and Tank.

"Don't tell me you're ordering a salad?" Evie smiled at Tracey who shook his head.   Evie silently smiled.

"No! Please don't! Get something else!" Tracey's laugh caused Evie to laugh harder.

"Okay...I'll have the angel hair pasta with pink salmon in the pepper sauce..." Evie paused looking at Tracey. "And a house salad, with ranch on the side." Tracey stared at Evie as Kim wrote down her order. Evie caught his eyes staring at her.

"Okay! And you sir?" Kim looked Tracey's way. "I would like a 20-ounce Prime Ribeye, medium-well. I'll also have a large baked potato with everything on it except for bacon, and an order of fried apples and fried sweet potatoes." Tracey flipped the page on the menu.

"Will that be all, sir?" Kim looked at Tracey contemplate, and then placed down the menu.

"Yes ma'am. And, if you could bring our drinks that will be great!" Tracey requested while examining Evie with his light brown eyes. Sheila talked to Tank, glancing at Evie while Kim took away their menus and walked away.

"You have a big appetite, don't you?" Evie questioned Tracey.

"A big man likes to eat big!" Tracey stared at her lips. He slid closer to Evie, placing his right arm on the back of her seat. Evie's curly hair stuck out of her high ponytail. Tracey gazed at her hair.

"Now getting back to what you need." Tracey licked his lips.

"Tell me more about the business and the position you're offering me?"

"I have many employees and many businesses located across the state. When we get finished eating, I will take you to one of them. Afterward, you can tell me if this is something you would like to do." Tracey eyed Evie with a smile, while she chuckled.

"Okay, but what is that telling me? You still haven't told me what type of position this job is!"

"Be patient." Tracey touched her chin. Sheila glanced over at them and rolled her eyes back towards Tank.

"You'll see. I can show you better than I can tell you." Tracey continued to flirt. Sheila and Tank remained deep into their conversation. Their drinks arrived.

"I need to wash my hands." Evie signaled Tracey to let her out from the booth. "Will you all excuse me?" Tracey stood up letting Evie out. Sheila looked at Evie's butt as she stood.

"Do your thing, ma." Tank chuckled looking at Sheila who smiled and stared at Evie. She strutted down the aisle headed to the lady's room. Tracey watched Evie's butt cheeks sway back and forth.

"Dang! I didn't know she had it like that!" Tank admired.

"She is gorgeous." Tracey commented to Sheila who took a sip of

her drink. Taking out a sealed packaged, Shelia opened it and slipped white powder in her drink, and then into Evie's Arnold Palmer.

"What are you doing?" Tank questioned Sheila, while looking at her with a mean face.

"You know how we do these ho's we meet! Why are you trippin'?" Sheila questioned him. Tracey looked at Tank and signaled him to shut up. Tank showed anger as he sipped his drink.

"Tracey what do you think about Evie?" Sheila questioned.

"You did real... good! Real... real good!" Tracey responded as Sheila held out her hand.

"I got you! Once she's hired, I'll pay you." Tracey reinsured.

"So that's tonight! After old girl drinks this . . ." Sheila picked up the glass, stirring the powder in Evie's glass.

"She's going to be feeling real nice!" With confidence Sheila spoke. Tracey smiled.

"No doubt! Once we leave here, I'm going to take her to the club to meet the other ladies. She doesn't know the treat she's in for. But she'll enjoy it." Nonchalant, Tracey picked up his drink and sucked from the straw.

"Sheila, take Tank where he needs to go, and we'll hook up later man!" Tracey grinned at Tank who rolled his eyes.

"All I need is a few hours. . ." The server interrupted Tracey with their food.

"Change the subject." Tracey looked up to Evie walking back to the table.

◆ ◆ ◆ ◆ ◆

After they finished dining, Tracey took Evie to one of his strip clubs to view the position he was offering her. By this time Evie was drugged, feeling nice and mellow. They arrived at the club. People were walking in and out, as the bass of the music thumps through the doors. Evie walked in first, while Tracey held the door for her. Evie's eyes lit up from all the bizarre women, half nude and nude. Evie observed the two stages with gold, shiny poles. On one stage, a girl danced exotically on the lit, clear, fiberglass stage. On the other stage, another dancer jumped to the top of the pole, sliding her body from upside down.

Tracey took Evie's hand while other women observe them. They sat at the round table in front of the stage. Tracey called two other girls over to meet Evie. The two dancers got up from the table across the stage. They walked toward Tracey. One dancer stopped to fix her white thigh-high boots. She bent over then proceeded toward Evie and Tracey.

"Evie, I would like you to meet Tira and Sonny." Tracey smiled.

"Hello," Evie waved with a smile, feeling good and high. Tira looked Evie up and down, and then waved back with attitude.

"Oh, she is real cute!" Sonny flirted. Tira looked at Sonny with a mean face.

"You better check yourself, quick!" Tira stared at Sonny with steamy eyes.

100

"Y'all ladies take that mess somewhere else." Tracey shoed Tira and Sony away, with an irritated demeanor. Tira rolled her eyes at Evie, grabbing Sonny's hand and switched to the other side of the club, pulling her along. Evie glanced at Tira from behind. Tira turned around staring eye to eye with Evie. She swung her long ponytail, rolled her eyes, and walked out of sight.

"Come on." Tracey stood up, taking Evie's hand. Grabbing his hand, she followed. As they walked through the champagne room, into a private VIP room, Evie observed a large, platinum pole with colorful lights all around. The music bumped as a spotlight maneuver all around the room.

"I want you to audition for me." Tracey stared at Evie.

"Okay!" Lustfully responding, Evie eyed Tracey up and down. Tracey walked up to Evie.

"Let me help you." Tracey began to undress her. Brown fingertips unbuttoned her blouse, she stared while he licked his lips. Tracey brushed his finger against her breast and down to her toned stomach. Evie's red pantie struck his eyes by mesmerized. He admired his favorite color. Evie released her hair from the ponytail and began to run her fingers through her long curly black hair. Barefoot she stepped on the stage. Evie danced like a professional.

Tracey observed closely, viewing every curve on her body. It moved to every rhythm. Tracey walked towards Evie on the stage. She looked into his eyes with full attraction, while grooving to the music. Tracey pulled her close. Evie looked up at Tracey who stood 6' 3". He embraced her while her face leaned against his chest. Tracey lowered his head, their lips touched. His brown fingertips unsnapped her red lace bra. Evie slowly slipped down her pantie. Tracey freed himself from his shirt, dropped his

denims and checkered boxers. Grabbing her waist, he picked Evie up, who wrapped her legs around him. Leaning his body against the gold pole, Tracey pressed himself in deep. Evie breathed in deep, grabbed his neck tight with one hand and the gold pole with the other, riding. He stroked.

Meanwhile, Tira is looking for Tracey. She walked through the champagne room, asking two of her co-workers of his whereabouts. They directed her to the private room. Tira walked toward the door with a drink in her hand. The sound of moaning outweighed the music. Tira listened. She grabbed the unlocked doorknob and slowly peeked in, watching Tracey and Evie. Anger displayed on her face, Tira looked at Evie with furious jealousy in her eyes.

◆◆◆◆◆

Tracey supplied everything Evie needed, in order to start working at the club, including advance pay. The next day, he purchased a condo to put her in that was fully furnished. Filled with joy, Evie twirled around in the middle of the marbled livingroom floor. Passionately, she kissed Tracey who smiled. "Grab your purse. Let's ride out. I wanna take you somewhere." Evie smiled at Tracey, grabbing her purse. They walked down a flight of stairs, into the garage. Tracey opened the door for Evie, she stepped in and closed the door. She stared at him as he walked to the driver side door.

"Tracey, I want to thank you so much for all of this!" Tracey pressed started, the engine rumbled upon Evie's smile.

"No need to thank me! I am a gentleman. You take care of me! I take care of you! And you pretty thing, is going to make us a lot of money!" Evie smiled at his statement. "Ready to ride?" Evie kissed his lips with a smile. "Let's ride!" Tracey smiled at Evie, shifting into reverse, and then they drove off.

Evie reclined her seat feeling like a princess, as she watched music videos on the TV dashboard. Tracey's chromed wheels of his Bentley, reflected on the glass window of the Mercedes Benz showroom. He pulled into a parking space.

"Are you buying another car?" Evie questioned with a smile.

"I am!" Tracey smiled back and placed his car in park. After shutting off the ignition, they both got out. Tracey looked around at the various vehicles around him, contemplating on which one he liked. Evie smiled as he stared at her full juicy lips.

"Your beauty is like a fragrance of essence that sings to my heart every time I look at you." Evie blushed and leaned in to kiss him, with a pause.

"Is that the same line you use with all of the ladies?" Tracey smiled at her, and then kissed her on the forehead. "Nah...only you baby!" Evie smiled back and kissed him.

"Okay, let's see...what should I get this time? A convertible, a coupe... what do you think Miss Evie?"

"I don't know!" Evie's eyes spotted an octave blue, Mercedes GLS 450.

"Well, I like that one!" Evie pointed and stared, walking towards it. She peeked through the driver's side window. A salesman walked behind Tracey.

"Hi, my name is Tom. Are you in the market for a car today?" the salesman introduces himself.

"We would like to test-drive this one." Tracey requested.

"Absolutely! Let me get the keys." Tom walked toward the front of the dealership. Meanwhile, Tracey walked up to Evie and kissed her with a smile.

"Okay, I'm back!" Tom held the keys in his hand.

"Who is test-driving the vehicle?" Tom looked at Tracey and Evie.

"My girl!" Tracey looked at Evie. Tom gave Evie the keys.

"Tracey, I . . ." Tracey interrupted by placing his finger on Evie's lips.

"You drive." Evie looked at Tracey, shook her head with a smile and rolled her eyes. She goes into her purse, took out her wallet and gave Tom her ID.

"Thank you." Tom made a copy of Evie's license, and then gave it back to her. She placed it inside of her purse. Tom unlocked the doors with the remote. Evie opened the door, admiring the bone-colored leather interior. Falling in love instantly, she sniffed the new car smell. Evie pressed start the ignition. Tom got into the vehicle while Tracey sat in the back. Evie pressed the buttons on the touch screen radio, turning up the volume to her favorite. The car's surround sound system amazed Evie. "Do you hear that bass? Man!" Tracey smiled along with Tom who explained all of the qualities of the vehicle. Evie drove off. They cruised around the block. Evie imagined herself in the vehicle driving herself to school. Finally, they arrived back to the dealership. Evie turned into the parking lot and placed the vehicle into parked.

"What do you think?" Tracey stared at Evie for a response.

"It's tight! I like it." Tom looked at Evie with a smile, as she grabbed her purse and stepped out of the vehicle. "Okay, we'll take it!" Tracey announced his decision to the salesman, who smiled with joy.

"Great! Let's walk back to my office." Tom led the way back into the building, and then into his office. He sat and pulled out a black binder, looking up that particular model.

"Okay the price of this GLS 450 fully loaded, including tax is $60,340." Tom gave Tracey the figures and handed him an application. "First, I will need to pull your credit to determine what the requirements would be."

"No need! I'm paying cash!" Tom's face lit up to Tracey's response.

"Cash!" Tom reiterated while looking at Tracey, who pulled out a roll of $10,000 bills. He counted.

"Well, just fill out sections one and two of the application. We don't take cash. But there's a bank right next door that gives cashier's checks to our customers."

"Great! About how long will all of this take?" Tracey looked at Tom. "Once the application is completed, and we received your payment, about 30 minutes." Tom replied.

Evie looked at the money Tracey held in his hand, thinking to herself. "Man, that's power being able to give up cash like that!" Evie had flash backs of her Uncle Gene who gave her money for the exchange of sex. Immediately, Evie shook those disgusting

thoughts out of her head. "What's wrong?" Tracey questioned looking at her.

"Just a slight headache." Evie shamefully looked at him.

"Oh, I have something for that! I'll give it to you in a minute. But for now, here's $70,000. Take this money next door to the bank and get a cashier check for $60,340." Tracey handed Evie the money with instruction. She counted out seven, $10,000 bills in her hand, mesmerized.

"I didn't know they made a bill this large." Evie folded the money and placed it inside her purse.

"You're going to learn a lot from me, Miss Evie" Tracey leaned over and kissed her lips in confidence. She grinned.

"Go ahead and handle that for me beautiful, so we can go. I have another appointment to get to."

"Okay!" Evie responded with a smile walking out of the sales office. Tracey watched Evie from behind until she exited the building.

Meanwhile, Tracey filled out the application and gave it to Tom. Before he knew it Evie had returned with the cashier's check. Tracey completed the deal and handed Tom the envelop.

"Looks like we are all set!" Tom handed Tracey the remote box.

"It was great doing business with you both. Enjoy your new vehicle." Tom congratulated.

"Sincerely! And thank you sir." Tracey and Evie shook their salesman's hand, and then they walked out holding hands.

"Here Evie." Tracey gave her the keys. Evie looked at them rather surprised.

"Oh, you want me to follow you. Sure!"

"No! I want you to park it in your garage and in a few weeks, go pick up your tags." Tracey gazed into Evie's eyes, handing her the paperwork. Evie stood speechless.

"What are you talking about Tracey?" Evie looked at him strangely.

"This vehicle belongs to you!" Tracey confessed.

"What! Stop playing! Tracey, are you for real?" Evie stared at her new vehicle with joy. Tracey smiled, watching her rejoice. She hugged him tightly, giving him a passionate kiss!

"Oh, my gosh! I don't know what to say!" Tracey dug into his right pocket, pulled it out and balled up his fist.

"Here, open your hand! This is a little something for your headache." He placed two dime size bags of marijuana in her hand. Evie smiled.

"Oh thanks! I guess I will need this for my first night at the club." Evie placed the bag of weed in her bra. "You go on and rest in your new place, and I'll see you at the club later." Evie wrapped her sleeveless smooth arms around Tracey's neck, he grabbed her

waist. Her hands caressed his head and her lips kissed over his. "Okay baby, we can continue this later! I have to go and handle some business." Tracey kissed her one more time strongly on the lips. Evie closed her eyes. Tracey smiled and walked to his white Bentley. Evie hopped into her new ride, started it up as Tracey blew his horn and he drove off. Evie tooted her horn, driving away with full of joy.

"Wow, this can't be true! I must be dreaming!" Evie told herself blowing her horn on purpose. "I have a horn. This is great! Thank you, God!" Evie opened her double sunroof. The breeze blew inside as she drove.

◆◆◆◆◆

Evie hasn't been to school in a week. Finally, she decided to go back to school the next day to flex her new ride. She arrived late, approached the main office for her late pass and ran into Mrs. Thompson.

"Evie, just the person I'd like to see! I've been looking for you all week. After what happened, I felt bad for not believing you. But when I called the number in your file that evening a lady answered. She said that you no longer live there and don't call there every again!" Mrs. Thompson shared in a lower tone.

"She called you a tramp and hung up on me!" Evie looked embarrassed as Mrs. Thompson looked at Evie with suspense.

"You haven't been in school for a week Evie. What is going on?" Evie looked strange at Mrs. Thompson, ignoring her. Evie looked away.

"I'm your teacher! I have the right to know what's going on at home!"

108

"No! You don't need to be in my business like that lady! All of a sudden you're concerned," Mrs. Thompson looked rather frustrated by Evie's remark. "I'm concerned about you, and this is how you disrespectfully speak to me?" Mrs. Thompson shook her head.

"Oh no, young lady! I will not tolerate this! Come on, we are going to the principal's office." Aggressively Mrs. Thompson grabbed Evie's arm. "Are you crazy?! Get your hands off me! You're not my mother!" Evie forcefully demanded Mrs. Thompson. Evie stared angrily.

"I've been hurting my entire life! I sat in your classroom with a black eye as swollen as a grapefruit. And you didn't believe anything that I told you. Then, you put on this front like you care, then you threaten to take me to the principal's office. Whatever!" Evie boldly stated looking away.

"You told me that you fell off your uncle's bike." Mrs. Thompson reminded Evie. "Is this story really true Evie?"

"It doesn't matter what I told you!" Evie responded in a smart tone. "Yes, it does!" Mrs. Thompson insisted as Evie shook her head in disbelief.

"No! It doesn't! Because I quit! I'm signing myself out! I don't need school, nor do I need a phony and stinky breath teacher like you in my face." Evie gave Mrs. Thompson attitude.

"You can't sign yourself out because you're not 18. A parent must give you approval." Her teacher stated. "Watch me! I don't have parents! They left me when I was eight. So as far as I am concerned, I'm grown! I haven't had parents for almost 10 years, and like hell, I don't need them now!" Evie rolled her eyes and

109

walked away. Mrs. Thompson stood in front of the office in shocked. The power of money lured Evie away from her dreams and goals. She decided that she will work full-time at the strip club. After signing herself out, Evie went back home, chilled and smoked a blunt on her balcony. Pushing her past to the back of her mind, Evie relaxed preparing herself for work that night.

◆◆◆◆◆

The telephone rang in room 666. Evie remained unresponsive. The phone continued to ring, but Evie doesn't move.

◆◆◆◆◆

Evie's cell phone rang at her new condo. "Hello," Evie answered while blowing weed smoke into the air.

"Hey Evie, it is Sheila!"

"What's up?" Evie questioned as she wiggled her French-pedicured toes, holding the blunt in her hand.

"I see my boy hooked you up!"

"Oh yeah, he hooked a 'sista' up for real" Evie responded to Shelia.

"So, tonight is your big night?" Sheila questioned in a jealous tone.

"Yes! And believe it or not, I'm not afraid! Since I was a little girl, I've always wanted to dance, but I never thought it would be in this way!" Evie babbled the conversation along.

"Well, I have to go. Hopefully, I will see you later." Evie picked up on Shelia's short tone.

"Sheila, is everything okay?" "I'm cool! I got to go." Sheila hung up in Evie's ear. Evie looked at the phone, hunched her shoulders and placed her phone next to her. Walking through her patio doors and into her bedroom, Evie went into her walk-in closet. She picked out whatever she dreamed of wearing, thinking to herself.

"Maybe it's not bad after all that my parents are missing! If my dad is with Keisha, oh well! I feel sorry for my mom but, she'll get over it wherever she is!" Evie abnormally reasoned from the effects of the marijuana. Picking out the sexiest outfit for work, Evie walked into the shower area and turned on the water. The steam began to heat up the bathroom while she walked back into her room. Through her bedroom doors, Evie ran down her bone-white colored, carpeted stairs. Her bare feet embraced each step, as she ran down, until landing at the bottom.

Evie turned on her surround sound. Disco music thumped loudly while her body grooved to the music. Feeling beautiful, she stood in the presence of her newly furnished living room, in front of her 32" x 18" gold framed mirror located over her fireplace. Evie danced. She began taking off her tank shirt, leaving her gray sports bra on. Sliding off her booty shorts, Evie danced like she was on stage. Evie glided around her living room, landing in a squat.

She bounced her booty cheeks, to the right, then to the left. As she stood in an upright position to the beat, Evie twirled around landing in a split. Placing both hands on the fresh scented carpet, she slightly pushed herself up enough to slide her forward leg back. Her muscles displayed through her biceps. Evie rolled over on her back, seductively bending her legs in an upright position.

She leaned back on her elbows for support, and she opened her leg. Dropping her head back, her left arm extended, as she rubbed her hands between her legs. She lifted her head forward while her

111

wild, curly black hair hung on her neck. The song goes off. The radio station went into commercial, as the fire alarm goes off upstairs. Evie forgot about the running hot water that she left on. The steam circulated into the hallway from Evie's room. She looked up and saw the steam gliding through the air, like smoke. She ran up the stairs and into her bedroom, shutting the door behind her.

Chapter Nine
The Mouth of Hell Widens

Mr. and Mrs. Klein were having bible study in their bedroom together. Suddenly, the Spirit of God spoke to Bishop Klein while he was having a discussion with his wife.

"Son, pray fervently for your daughter Sheila. Death is on its way to her. Begin to pray for laborers to go forth on her behalf. Pray that her heart opens to receive My son Jesus and that she comes back to Me. When you have done that, Sheila's blood will no longer be on your hands. You will have done, all that I have spoken. Her chances are narrowing. Continue to obey Me, and I will release the pain off of your heart. I will heal you both." The Spirit of the God spoke.

"Honey." Bishop looked at his wife. "The Lord just spoke to me, and He said we must pray fervently for our daughter now."

"Kenneth." Deborah looked strange at her husband.

"We must pray for Evie too. That's the young lady I mentioned to you earlier. The Lord just flashed a vision of Sheila and Evie." His wife stated. Kenneth took his wife by the hand.

"Come on, we're going into our prayer closet." Bishop stood to his feet sternly.

"I'll be damned, if we allow Satan to take our only daughter without a fight!"

"Honey..." Deborah stared at Kenneth a slight grin. "You just cussed!"

"Forgive me." He addressed his wife, pausing with tears in his eyes. "I repent Lord." Kenneth pauses, as tears fall from the corner of his eyes.

"It's just." Kenneth startled from the pain that he felt. He sat back down and leaned towards his wife, laying his head on his wife's chest.

"I am hurting Deborah. I just lost my mother three months ago, and my father died 10 years ago, when I first stepped into ministry. Now the enemy is trying to rob us of our daughter." He lamented. Tears fell from his eyes, Deborah held him close. He released the heaviness from his heart while Deborah rests her hand, on his head.

"She's our only baby girl. I am angry Deborah. I'm angry at Satan." Kenneth sat up, while his wife wiped his face.

"The righteous anger of the Lord is rising for the evil in this world. People, including our daughter doesn't realize the stronghold that Satan has on them. They think what they are doing is a lifestyle and normal. But they are being tricked by the trickster! The lust of money and their selfish lifestyle will take them out of this world.

"You are right honey." Deborah looked into her husband's eyes with sadness. "God has given people choices. He did not create robots. He wants people to willingly obey and serve Him, so He can be the protector over their lives. But if they choose to live their lives according to their own free-will, full of pleasure and act as if God doesn't exist. God will give them those desire of their hearts.

114

"I don't mean to sound cruel. Your reality is the reflection of your choices. When young adults, even adults, choose not to listen to that inner man for guidance, they will reap the consequences of what they've chose. And when there is a struggle of listening to your intuition, God will send you a messenger. If that message is rejected, destruction comes next." Kenneth nodded his head to his wife's statement.

"You are right honey and people would rather give in to the lust of their flesh! The Bible talks about that. But as soon as things don't go their way, folks blame God, especially when they see their entire life descending into a disaster. Hell is real!" Kenneth cracked a grin at his wife as she swung her feet to the floor to stand. Kenneth stood up.

"Let's be obedient and go into prayer now. God has shown us the plans of the enemy for our daughter and Evie. Now we must go fight those spirits that want to destroy their lives. Once we have fought the good fight of faith through prayer, the rest is up to God. Our daughter must want to walk in righteousness. Evie must want to walk with God! No, I don't want to see anything happen to our daughter or Evie. Deborah spoke with authority.

"But for Sheila, if she continues to walk away from God, the devil will claim her soul. The Lord will turn her over to a reprobate mind just because she turned her soul over to the devil first. God will send His angels to minister to her before destruction devours her. The rest is up to Sheila, Kenneth." Deborah continued to minister to husband. Kenneth cracked a smile.

"I love you and I thank God for a woman like you." Kenneth kissed and hugged his wife. They both walked together into their huge walk-in closet and shut the door behind them.

◆◆◆◆◆

The hotel clerk tried calling Evie in Room 666, to make her aware of her noonday checkout time. Her phone continued to ring. No answer.

◆◆◆◆◆

Evie answered the telephone while driving to the club.

"Hello." Evie picked up the phone.

"Hi, beautiful." Tracey flattered her.

"Hey Tracey." Evie smiled while she kept her eyes on the road.

"Are you on your way to the club."

"I am." Evie turned down her music.

"Listen, I may not be there tonight, but Tank will. He'll instruct you once you get there." Tracey stated.

"I hope he doesn't try to push up on me like you did." Evie laughed at her statement.

"Nah, he won't." Tracey reinsured.

"But... if he does, I am pretty sure you'll enjoy it." Tracey sarcastically spoke with a laugh.

"What do you mean by that?" Evie attitude shifted to offense.

"Exactly, what I said!" Tracey arrogantly spoke.

"Oh so, you think you've done something for me that permits you to talk to me any kind of way?" Evie clicked the Bluetooth, hanging up on him.

"Ooh! Something told me this was too good to be true." Evie stopped at the red light in frustration, hitting the steering wheel. Meanwhile, Tracey called Tank.

"Yo' man, do me a favor tonight?" Tracey instructed Tank, driving with his seat laid back, as his watch bling to the streetlights.

"Keep an eye on Evie. Make sure she doesn't leave the club before her time. She is scheduled from nine tonight, until seven in the morning. I'll hit you up later, straight!"

"Gotcha man!" Tank agreed.

"Cool! I need to satisfy an issue that's hounding me, you feel me?" Tracey chuckled.

"Handle your business!" Tank spoke not thrilled.

"Okay man, I'll give you a call later on." Tracey stated.

"Cool" Tank hung up and walked back into the club. Evie arrived at the club, driving her vehicle to the front for valet parking. The chaperon walked up to her while she placed it in park. He opened the door for Evie, taking her by the hand. She stepped out.

"Man, too bad I am out here working because I would sure tip you well." The chaperon commented. Evie gave him a disgusted look. He took her black suitcase out of the trunk.

"Good thing you are working out here. I would not let you touch me with a grill like that!" Evie thought to herself.

"If anything, I need to give you a tip and go get your teeth fixed." Evie faked a smile, grabbing her suitcase and rolled it to the entrance of the club. She walked into security. They thoroughly checked her and her bag. Afterward, Evie signed in. Sonny stood at the front with another girl, helping security check people in.

"Officer, I'll search her for you" Sonny looked at Evie who made a mean face and rolled her eyes.

"Excuse me, you have the wrong one. I don't get down like that." Evie spoke with attitude.

"Just ignore her." The masculine officer looked at Evie and stated.

"If anything, a man needs to search her. And I am not talking about in this way." The officer stated looking at Sonny.

"What! Say something." He stated to Sonny who rolled her eyes, got up, and walked back into the club area.

"Keep an eye on her and her lover. If you have any trouble, you let me know" Evie smiled at the officer's statement. "Thank you!" She grinned.

"By the way, you are a cutie!" The officer commented grabbing her hand and smiling. Evie smiled suspiciously, pulling her hand back and entered the club. She walked through, observing the many girls working hard. Some lapped danced, while others were on stage working the poles.

"How can I be different and make more money than the rest of these chicks?" Evie questioned herself. While she walked to the dressing room, she stared at Tira on stage. With her back turned, Tira noticed Evie from the back. She rolled her eyes and continued her set as the music thumped throughout the club. The men cheer Tira on. Evie entered the dressing room. There's an older, brown-lady, sitting on a tall bar stool in front of a counter with all types of feminine products. Powers, oils, cologne, outfits, tampons. and condoms are displayed around her.

"Hey baby, I am Helen. The ladies call me momma Helen. I am the dressing room house mom. Tank told me some new faces were coming aboard. I assume you are one of them." Both ladies smiled at each other. "I am. My name is Evie."

"Well, it's a pleasure meeting you, Evie. While you're working, I'll keep an eye on your things. At the end of your shift, you must tip out the D.J $20 and $15 goes to me. I am very certain that you won't have any problems making money here. You are gorgeous!" The house mom gazed at Evie, eyeing her fitted blue jeans.

"You're blessed like me! See!" Momma Helen stood up, poking out her butt. "Oh yeah, you are at the right place." The men here like fat asses! And that my friend you got! Helen sat back down on her tall high stool. Evie bashfully smiled at her statement.

"Okay!" Evie replied while taking a deep breath and widened her brown eyes with a smile. "Well...Thanks!" Evie walked into the locker room searching for an empty one, pulling her black suitcase along the side her.

"There were too many females looking at each other." Evie thought, secluding herself from the other dancers. She walked to the other side toward the bathroom, running into Sonny, who looked at Evie with strong attraction. Quickly, Evie walked into

the lady's restroom, locking the stall. She sat on the toilet and began to cry uncontrollably. She rested her elbows on her legs and her hands on her face. "How did I get here, and what have I gotten myself into? I am not a stripper!" Evie realized, as she kicked the bathroom door.

"Damn it!" In frustration she vented.

"Girlfriend?! Are you okay in there?" A voice came from the next stall.

"I am fine." Evie responded in a teary voice. She got up and goes into her roller suitcase to get out her first outfit. As she is undressing, she overheard a male calling her name.

"Is Evie in here?" Tank questioned the other ladies. Sonny overheard.

"I saw her walking toward the bathroom." Tank looked at Sonny with a laugh and shook his head.

"Of course, the woman hunter would know." Sarcastically Tank commented while Sonny smiled with a lollipop in her mouth. "You know it!" Sonny replied in confident. Tank walked into the women's bathroom calling Evie's name. The young lady who was talking to Evie jumped back into the bathroom, upon her exiting.

"Evie are you in here?" Tank looked around.

"I'm in here. I'll be out in 10 minutes." Evie displayed a puzzled face, took a breath, and shook her head.

"Hurry up! You are up at nine o'clock, okay?" Tank reminded.

"Got it!" Evie confirmed while laying her brown, fitted shirt on top of her suitcase.

"When you come out, go straight to the DJ booth and select your songs."

"Well, I have my own CD." Evie responded.

"Great! Just, put your name on it and give it to the DJ. Okay ma?" Tank smiled at the closed stall.

"Okay." Evie sat on the toilet with her jeans halfway off, as she unzips her brown, knee-length, skinny-heeled boots. Tank walked off his footsteps fade. Two seconds later, the blonde Caucasian girl exited the stall, and walked over to the tall skinny mirror to look at herself.

She placed her red finger nailed hands on her breasts lifting them from the inside her gold shimmered exotic bra top. Evie exited the stall pulling her suitcase behind her. She then placed it on the side of the stall door. The Caucasian girl looked at her through the mirror.

"Hi, my name is Seduction." Evie took a couple of steps forward and shook her extended hand.

"Evie." Stated her name.

"Evie is your stage name?" Seduction questioned while she fixed her blonde curly hair.

"No, Evie is my name." Evie fixed her straight jet-black hair, looking at herself in the mirror.

"Well girlfriend, from one stripper to another give yourself a stage name! Don't disclose your government name." Seduction suggested.

"Get a stage name!" Evie smiled at Seduction while she took out a clear bag with white powder. Dipping her pinky into it, Seduction scooped a small portion and sniffed it through her right nostril. Holding the left nostril, she tilted her head back and sniffed. Seduction then wiped her nose.

"Do you want some? You need to be high dealing with these fools."

"I'm straight! Thank you tho." Evie firmly responded, walking in her six-inch stilettos, and strutting to the front of the dressing room. Evie glanced at some of the girls. A tall dark chocolate female with an afro ponytail looked Evie up and down, and then rolled her eyes giving her a dirty look. "Can I check my stuff in?" Evie looked at the house mom.

"Sure baby!" Helen looked at Evie with a smile as she displayed frustration from the different vibes she was receiving. Evie looked around.

"If I can endure everything my life has gone through, I can deal with these jealous chicks up in here!" Evie thought to herself while rolling her eyes and turning her head. Her silk jet black hair slung.

"You go girl. I like that." Helen glanced at Evie's elegant black silk sheer, exotic wear.

"I really like that! I also make costumes." Helen informed Evie.

"After you complete your sets, come back here and take a look at some of the outfits I have." The house mom pointed to all of her exotic garments.

"I'll be sure to do that." Evie responded with a grin and strutted out the dressing room, into the club area. All eyes were on Evie while she walked past the platform stage. Two girls were doing their thing on separate stages. Evie walked up three flights of stairs toward the DJ booth.

"Hi, here's a Neo-Soul and R&B mixed CD." Evie smiled while giving her CD to the DJ.

"Hi, my name is C-Low." The stocky Hispanic smiled giving her a pen.

"Write your name on your CD. At the end of the nigh.t you can pick it up here. Evie grabbed the pen and wrote her name on the inside case. "What is you stage name?" C-Low asks Evie. She hunches with a smile.

"Don't be like some of these dancers up in here and give yourself a stupid name. Name yourself something that best describe you." C-Low looked at Evie contemplate on what name to write. C-low glanced a. her daydream he smiled.

"Pretty momma." C-Low called Evie with a smile.

"What would I call myself?" Thinking quickly, Evie thought.

"The hidden tears of pain trapped in my heart and the day I get the good news about my family; I can release them like an ocean wave."

"Yeah, that's it! Ocean!" Evie smiled at her decision. C-Low waved his hands in Evie's face.

"Yoo-hoo! I don't have all night you're on in one minute.

"What . . ." before C-Low can finish Evie interrupted with a smile.

"Ocean." Evie wrote on her CD. C-Low smiled with a nodding of his head.

"Yeah... I like that! You're fine as hell like an Ocean." C-Low complimented Evie. He stood from his tall, black stool leaning inward, grabbing the microphone. "Thank you!" Evie responded while giving him back his pen. She clapped her hands along with the crowd, cheering for the dancer on the stage.

"Can you play numbers two and five!" Evie requested. "How many sets am I doing?" Evie asked C-Low.

"Six." C-low replied.

"Okay, play numbers two, five, six, eight, eleven and twelve."

"Got it! And you're on in . . ." C-Low counted down from 10, as Evie walked toward the stage. "I would like to introduce our newest dancer to the stage, Ocean! Show your love!" C-Low hyped up the crowd! Without fear, Evie stepped onto the stage. The crowd of men roared in lust whistling and applauding. She looked

around. Observing her surroundings, she noticed familiar faces of several celebrities. She danced like a professional. Money rained on the stage. Evie unbuttoned the only button on her long elegant sheer exotic wear. She slipped it off, sliding it across the stage.

Leaving her bra top on, Evie rubbed her small waist down to her sexy, honey-brown thighs. The money flooded around her. She pulled up on the pole and slid herself down, landing into a split and pushed herself up and down with her fist. The men roared like lions. Twenty-dollar bills, fifties and hundred-dollar bills, hit the stage. Evie fell to her knees arching her behind in the air. Evie slowly dipped herself down, down, and further down, stopping while supporting herself with her left-hand. Placing her right hand on her hip, she dips toward the ground without touching it and popped up. She dipped and dipped, and then squatted to her knees; making her butt cheeks bounce one by one to the beat of the music.

Evie placed her legs against the pole. A tall dark-skinned man placed $100 at her feet, seductively licking his lips at her. Tira and Sonny sat right in front of the stage. Tira rolled her eyes at Evie. The dollar amount escalated with money all round her. The crowd applauded. Evie completed her first set. Entering into her second set, Evie picked up her money, while standing next to the gold pole. She placed it inside of her garter belt as continued to dance. Evie squatted down in various spots and continued to gather her money.

During her last set, she bended over to receive her tip, not knowing that Tira and Sonny were sitting right in front of her at a round table. Tira and Sonny talked over the noise, Evie overheard.

"I don't like her!" Tira replied with an attitude, while looking at Evie with dirty looks. "And... she won't give me no play!" Tira slapped Sonny from her statement.

"Don't make me cut you!" Tira threatened Sonny, who looked at her and laughed. "Lay off the Hennessy before you get hurt!" Sonny responded in a serious tone. "I need you to sneak out and get my gun." Tira insisted, giving Sonny $200.

"Here! Hit off the chaperon and keep a hundred. Just tell him that you left one of Milky Way's bag in the wine-colored Escalade." Angrily Tira spoke.

"That slut embarked on the wrong territory! I'll fix her. How dare she walk up in here thinking she's running things! There's only one queen who runs this house, and that's me! I got something for you! Tira sternly watched Evie dance. Both ladies locked eyes. Evie swung her black hair turning her butt toward Tira and smacked it, and then clapped it from side to side.

◆◆◆◆◆

After Evie overheard Tira and Sonny's conversation she played it off like she heard nothing. The music ended for her last set.

"Lets' give it up, one more time for Ocean!" C-Low announced. Calmly, Evie exited the stage and strutted quickly into the dressing room toward the house mom. Sweat dripped all over her body.

"Leave now!" The Spirit of God spoke to Evie., she walked with urgency.

"Don't leave. You need to make more money to pay Tracey back." A deceiving voice spoke confusing her. Evie shook her head back and forth, battling with the two voices, as she walked into the dressing room.

"Evie are you alright? You look flustered." Helen stared at Evie's

disturbed demeanor. Evie pranced back and forth. "I have to get the hell out of here! That girl Tira is crazy! I overheard her telling her lover, that she is coming for me. She's been rolling her eyes at me all night." Evie continued to prance in worry. Helen looked at Evie, and then grabbed both her arms. "Calm down. Look at me. Take deep breaths." Evie closed her eyes and inhaled, and then exhaled. She opened them to momma Helen who looked at her.

"Here I will pay you, but please help me to get out of here." Evie pulled her money out from her garter belt and counted it in front of Helen.

"Damn girl, you banked out there! That's why she is jealous. You bumped her from her throne, now you are the hottest new dancer in this club. How much is that?" Helen looked at Evie's money and questioned.

"$3,575.00!" Helen eyes widen to the amount. "Wow! And that was just your first set." Helen babbled. Evie looked around for her suitcase.

"Listen, here is your money and some extra. Please help me get out of here. Please?!" Evie begged, staring into Helen's eyes. Helen sighed counting three-hundred dollars, and then pulled Evie behind some curtains. "Okay. Your suitcase is right there. Get dress back here and look down?" Evie looked while Helen pointed to the sewage grate.

"This would be your best escape. It will lead you into the parking garage. It's not the best smelling exit, but it will get you out safe." Evie began to undress as Helen talked.

"Okay. Thank you so much." Helen looked at Evie with concern as she got dress quickly.

"You're welcome. I hope to see you again." Helen stated. Evie slipped on her boots. "I really doubt that. After tonight, I'm not sure what's going to happen to me." Evie squatted and shoved her clothes into the suitcase and then stood.

"Well…I'll be praying for you." Helen smiled at Evie, who moved over so Helen can remove the grate. Evie looked into the dark hole. "It looks dark down there." Helen stared at Evie who looked concerned.

"It is, but you'll be alright. There's a ladder against the wall. Just climb down until you meet your luggage at the bottom." Helen grabbed Evie's suitcase and dropped it down. Evie squatted, climbing into the sewage hole. Helen helped her. Once Evie was secured on the ladder, she began to climb down, and Helen closed the sewage grate. Helen smiled and walked through the curtains.

Chapter Ten
A Living Nightmare

The veins on both sides of Evie's head had increased in size from stress. Her head pounded. The only thing she thought about was going home and lying in her bed, as she ran in the parking garage. Pressing the panic button on her remote, Evie located her vehicle. She ran to it, threw her bag in the trunk, and then hopped in locking the doors. It started. Looking at the clock, it displayed 10:49 p.m. She cruised onto I-17 as her chrome-wheels reflected off the streetlights.

◆◆◆◆◆

Tira and Sonny walked into the dressing room looking for Evie. They asked around for her.

"House mom, have you seen the new girl?"

"Which one?"

"Ocean!" Tira responded with attitude.

"No! The last time I saw her, was when she first checked in. Other than that, I haven't seen her." Helen kept a serious face while she answered Tira. "Thank you! If you see her, don't tell her that we were looking for her. We'll find her." Tira gave Helen a fake smile. Sonny walked behind her as they exited the dressing room.

"Okay... I understand now! Them two..." Helen shook her head in disgust. "I don't blame you, Evie! I would run from them fools too! They are crazy." Helen babbled aloud.

Evie approached her condo. She decided to park in front of the house, instead of the garage. Getting out of the vehicle, she walked to the front door. The noise alarmed her while unlocking the door. Evie pushed it open and stood in the doorway.

"I know I wasn't that high when I left! I don't remember leaving my surround-sound on." Evie spoke out loud to herself. She walked up the stairs. The closer she got to the top the louder moaning sounds came from her bedroom. The door was slightly ajar. Evie peeked in and opened the door quietly without a squeak. She discovered sexual action through the dim lights of her bedroom!

"Aw, Tracey . . . Aw yeah . . ." Evie entered the bedroom in shocked.

"You like that!" Tracey spoke in a heavy breathing. Evie walked to the foot of the bed.

"Alexa, brighten the lights?!" The lights brightened. Tracey jumped up. Sheila looked at Evie by surprised. "Wow, this is real fouled! But I forgot, Tracey paid for all of this! So, does that mean, you can come in here anytime you please and bring whomever?" Evie questioned holding back her tears. Her mouth shivered.

"You supposed to be at the club!" Tracey responded in anger.

"Right! You stupid bastard!" Evie raged and stormed out.

"Damn!" Tracey attempted to run after Evie, but realized he was naked.

"Well Evie, someone else had to break this lovely bed in besides

130

you. You would still be broke, lost, and staying in cheap motels if it wasn't for Tracey and me! So, we celebrated." Sheila screamed out. Tracey zipped his pants and threw on his shirt.

"Just let her go. She'll be back! She needs us!" Sheila babbled while Tracey looked for his car keys.

"Shut up, Shelia, and get dressed!" Tracey slipped on his shoes, looking around the room for his keys.

"I'll meet up with you later. When you leave out, make sure you close the garage door." Tracey yelled, flying out the room and hopping two steps at a time until he reached the bottom. He walked through the kitchen and into the garage to his car. Tracey pressed the garage button on the wall, it opened, and then he got into the Bentley. In reverse he back out and then skids off. He speeded down the street, taking short cuts until he hopped on the Interstate. At 100 mph, Tracey spotted Evie in his right lane. He switched lanes, driving behind her.

"Call Tank." Tracey spoke, the phone rang.

"Hey man, what's up?" Tank answered.

"Tank!" Tracey boldly called his name.

"Yeah?" Tank replied through a noisy background!

"Go somewhere so you can hear me." Tracey spoke loudly. Tank walked outside.

"Okay, can you hear me now?"

"Where is Evie?" Tracey questioned.

"She's here." Tank responded in conference.

"Are you sure about that Tank?" Tracey angrily called his name.

"Yeah, man!" Tank suspiciously made a face on the other end of the phone.

"You're slipping Tank!"

"What man?!" Tank questioned in suspense.

"You are slipping Tank!" Tracey repeated himself in frustration.

"She's not in the club, Tank! I am following her now! And what I need to know from you is, how did that happen?"

"I don't know, man!" Tank answered in worry.

"I left you in charge and I gave you specific orders! How much money did she make?"

"I don't know. I didn't know she left the club!" Tank responded I distressed.

"You know what Tank?! I'll deal with you later. I'll handle this!" Tracey angrily hung up in Tank's ear. He opened his glove department. He took out his gun and placed it on the side of him. Tracey continued to follow Evie to her destination. Evie drove into one of the most expensive hotels she could find. Driving into the

parking lot of the hotel, she slammed the gear into park and hopped out. The door closed while Evie pushed it with her back. She chirped the alarm and ran into the hotel. Evie took out her ID and gave to the front desk attendant along with her credit card. She swiped it and then gave it back to Evie. Her receipt printed. In the meanwhile, Evie looked over her shoulder.

"Thank you." The attendant handed Evie a room key and receipt. Quickly, she walked toward the elevator, pressing the button. The doors opened. Evie jumped in, pressing number six.

"Go, go . . ." Evie spoke to the elevator, as the doors began to shut. Evie laid her head back on the gold-colored walls, breathing heavily. The elevator reached the six floor. Evie exited the elevator and turned the corner. Tracey popped out from the other side. Evie jumped and tried to scream. But Tracey placed his hand over her mouth, taking his gun out from underneath his shirt. Tracey slipped the gun down Evie's pants toward her vagina. He rubbed the chrome caliber against her private area.

"If you scream or try anything I don't like, I will blow your insides out. Understood!" Tracey threatened. Evie nodded her head. He pulled out the gun and they walked to Evie's room. Tracey's hand remained over her mouth. He looked behind himself. Upon reaching the room, tears fell from Evie's eyes, dripping on Tracey's hand. She opened the room door. They entered and Tracey kicked the door, it slammed.

◆◆◆◆◆

In the unseen world, God's angels are released on an assignment in the earth, prompting the intercessors to pray fervently. While the death angels go out, grabbing souls out of their earthly bodies and into a dark place. Sheila walked into a 24-hour grocery store and down the snack aisle. A beautiful light-complexioned woman, with a gold glitz in her skin and sandy-brown hair stood behind Sheila. Sheila bent down to get herself a bag of chips, stood and

133

turned around to the tall lady who towered over her. "Sheila." The strange lady addressed.

"Yes, and who are you?" Sheila questioned by surprised.

"An angel who stands before you with the following message from God." The angel pulled out a piece of paper. **"Sheila my daughter, I am calling you into repentance now. You must come to me and turn from your wicked ways. Death is thirsty for you and if you do not come, anger will consume you and death will open up and devour you. For I love you, and you are My chosen one. But I will allow your enemies to destroy you if you don't come to me NOW."** The angel repeated what the Spirit of God spoke.

"Sheila, for I Am Love. Please come to me now!" Sheila looked at the beautiful angel as if she were crazy. But she remained silent and listened.

"Sheila, for I am Patient, so come to Me now! Sheila, for I am Merciful so come to Me now! Sheila, I Am Forgiving so come to Me now! Sheila, for I Am of Joy, you must come to Me now! Sheila, I Am your Heavenly Father who is calling you into 'My Will' now! Sheila, I am the only one who will protect you from death after you walk out of this store. If you don't answer My call, you will not see tomorrow. For Your Heavenly Father is calling you now! Sheila, it's time to turn from your wicked ways. If you choose not to answer the Lord your God, all those who are praying for you will not be held accountable for your blood." Spoke the Spirit of the living God through the angel.

Sheila snatched the paper from her hand. "God didn't tell you that!" Sheila replied.

"Who sent you?! Did my father send you? He did, didn't he?! And, after I told him to leave me alone!" Sheila closed her eyes furious.

"Tell him that he better watch out for his church, because I'm going to destroy it!" When Sheila opened her eyes, the angel was gone. Sheila put down the chips and ran outside to see if she saw the angel. The only thing she saw was the darkness of the midnight hour and the streetlights of the parking lot.

"You can set your father's church on fire later. Just go back to the club and have a drink." Shelia's free-will desired.

◆◆◆◆◆

In room 666 Evie tossed and turned, trying to wake up. The last thing she remembered was Tracey in the bathroom of her hotel room, talking to Tank. "Man, ten minutes has passed! Where is the stuff I asked you to bring?" Tracey questioned Tank.

"I'm coming up on the elevator now." Tank told Tracey who clicked off his phone and walked out of the bathroom in his boxers. Evie laid in bed between the sheets naked. Tracey drugged her and sexually abused her. Her eyes were very glassy from the drugs.

"How's my ho, huh? Are you ready for the rest of your tube feeding?" Tracey laughed, taking the half-full needle from the nightstand and injected more drugs into her thigh. Evie moaned. The cocaine rushed through her veins. He grabbed her breast and slapped her.

"You like that don't you?" Evie laid silent, looking at Tracey through her drugged vision. The door knocked. Tracey walked over and let Tank in.

Chapter Eleven
The Death Angel

Bishop and Mrs. Klein walked out of the closet. It's 3 a.m. Kenneth got into bed, rolled over, prepared himself to go to sleep. "Goodnight, honey." Kenneth leaned over and kissed his wife.

"We both shall sleep peacefully without any worries. God has heard our prayers. So be it," Deborah smiled at her husband and rolled over to her side. She laid with her eyes opened, listening to the Spirit of God speak to her.

"Deborah, you can only call a child away from a fire, so they won't get burned. You can only call them again when they refuse not to listen. But it is only 'I' who has the power to keep them from being burned in a devouring fire. They shall burn from disobedience. Get up without tears and go into your closet and place the black suit on the bedroom door. The one that you preached in last year at the Women's Day Conference entitled, The Thief. I will wake my son up before you in the morning, and he will know what the suit on the door represents." Deborah slowly stood and walked into the closet and obey the spirit.

Walking into their closet, she took out the black suit and placed it on the bedroom door. Peacefully she hummed walking back to her bed, laid down and closed her eyes. Deborah rested her soul.

◆◆◆◆◆

Two hours later, Tracey had robbed Evie, both men had raped her, and then they exit room 666 , leaving her naked between the sheets.

◆◆◆◆◆

In the meanwhile, Sheila sat at the bar of the strip club drinking. The club had quieted down. People began to exit. A dark strong mist surfaced in the air, leaving the atmosphere dark and foggy. It seeped through the front door of the strip club where there were still numerous of women. Some sat around drinking, smoking cigarettes and cigars while others gave private dances.

Evil spirits hovered their way through the air of the club and attached themselves to Tira. She's possessed with sudden anger, slamming her drink on the bar. The shot glass shattered. Liquor spilled out. "That's it! Where is Evie, Sonny?!" Tira yelled walking towards Sonny. "What are you asking me for?" Sonny slurred her words.

"I was with Evie, I mean with you, all night!" Sonny hilariously laughed in Tira's face. Boiling in anger, Tira got up and walked all through the club, asking around for Evie. No one knew anything. Tira saw Sheila sitting on the other side of the club.

"She knows!" Tira thought to herself, walking up to Sheila. Approaching her closely.

"Where's your girl?" Tira asked with an attitude.

"And who may that be?" Sheila sipped on Vodka and Coke. "I have many of those, including you!" Sheila smirked. Tira rolled her eyes at her comment.

"Evie!" Sheila looked at Tire and laughed at her answer.

"I don't know. Go find her." Sheila turned her head away laughing, and then sipped her drink. Tira walked off toward Sonny. She

laughed at Tira and shook her head. "You're crazy!" Tira rolled her eyes at Sonny's statement.

"I'm about to show you crazy! I'm tired of playing games. So, this is what I need you to do. Locate the fuse box and flick off the electricity." Tira whispered to Sonny, who looked at her strange.

"Why, Tira? You are wilding out. Stop acting crazy!" Sonny looked at Tira for an explanation. "I'm looking for Evie and since everyone wants to act like they don't know, we're about to find her." Whispered Tira.

"What are you planning on doing Tira?" Sonny displayed a frustrated demeanor towards her. "Just do what I ask!" Sonny got up.

"Yeah, Mr. Security, you're first!" Tira walked toward the lobby. Before she could get there, the lights went out. Quickly she pulled her gun out of her thigh high boots, Tira fired all over the club until it was completely silenced. Sonny remained at the fuse box until it was quiet and then she ran out. Together, they escaped out the backdoor and down an alleyway.

"We need to hide somewhere quick!" Tira stated.

"What in the hell was that about? So, you killed innocent people because you couldn't find who you were looking for? You are straight up demonic!" Sonny yelled as they ran with a fast heartbeat.
"We're cool!" Tira calmly spoke , both, ladies quickly got into Tira's cherry colored escalade and drove off.

◆ ◆ ◆ ◆ ◆

Front desk continued to knock at Evie's hotel door. Finally, she

woke up and screamed, looking all around her. She sat up in a cold, wet bed. Knocking continued at the door. Evie looked down in the bed discovering that her body fluids had released everywhere.

"I think I am going to be sick!" Evie jumped up out of bed, placing her hand over her mouth while running into the bathroom. Vomit flew all over the toilet. The knocking continued, Evie grabbed a towel to wipe her mouth and hands, walking back into the room.

"Ma'am we need you to check out. We've been calling you." Evie looked at the clock, 8:10 a.m. displayed.

"What day is it?" Evie questioned herself, hallucinating and acting delirious. "How did I get here?" Yelling, she threw the bed linen off the bed. "Where are my clothes?" Evie looked around the room while the attendant eavesdrops.

"If you don't open up ma'am, I will be forced to call the police." The attendant stated. The knocking stopped. Evie spotted a hotel robe and covered her nakedness. She opened the front door and looked down the hallway, but no one was there. Evie closed the door and walked to the telephone. She dialed.

"Hello, this is Evie from room 666."

"Yes, we have been calling you since yesterday at noon. Your bill has rolled into another day." The front desk attendant stated.

"What is the amount?" Evie questioned, looking at her suitcase.

"$550.00." Front desk answered.

"Okay, can I pay by credit card over the phone?"

"Yes, you may." The front desk answered Evie.

"I really do apologize for the inconvenience. I've had a long life."
In sadness Evie spoke.

"Excuse me?" The attendant wasn't clear.

"I meant night. I've had a long night." Evie reiterated, placing her
hand over one of her eyes.

"Okay, Miss Young, we're ready for your card number." The
attendant requested as Evie looked around in frustration. "Let me
find my card and I'll call you back." Evie hung up on the
attendant. Needles, weed bags, bomb pipes, liquor bottles and
condoms, laid all over the room, Evie stared in distress.

"No!" Evie screamed. Her voice echoed in the room. Evie tried to
remember what had happened. Finally, it dawned on her when
Tracey met her off the elevator. Tears fell down her face, she
continued to remember more. Evie sat on the foot of the bed.
Tracey tried to kiss her, but she turned away. Evie remembered
more. Tracey slapped her and forced her to have sex with him.
Evie tried to scream, but Tracey placed his gun in her vagina and
threatened her. He flipped her over onto her stomach. He sat on
her back, holding her hands down while digging into his pocket.
He pulled out a needle with one hand and dug in the other pocket.
Pulling out a small bottle of liquid Heroin, Tracey filled the
needle. Evie lied still, while looking over her shoulder, questioning
him.

"Why are you doing this to me?" Evie cried.

"You don't question your boss! You wanted a job, so I hired you, to do as I said. And you didn't. Now you pay." Tracey filled the needle. "Now you leave me no other choice other than to make you cooperate." Tracey rammed the needle in her thigh. The thought made Evie jump, placing her hand on her thigh as she looked down at the bruise from the needle. Evie rubbed it, noticing a knot. She remembered crying as the needle stayed in her thigh until it was empty. Evie stood up and threw the pillows off the bed and pulling the sheets. She screamed. The tears stormed down her face.

"What have they done to me?" Evie screamed out.

"I have been born and turned into trash!" Hysterically Evie cried out, walking over to her purse. Angrily looking and moving things around, she saw her lip-gloss, brush, and license. "Where are my keys and money?" Evie broke down crying, looking around the room and throwing things.

"Why didn't I place my spare key back in my suitcase?" Evie threw her bag across the room. She ran her fingers through her hair. It began to curl back to its natural texture. Walking over to her boots, she picked up one and walked into the kitchen to get a butter knife out of the drawer. She took it and turned her boot upside down and pried open its bottom. $3,000 laid flat in the soles of the boot.

"This is enough money for a bus ticket and a couple weeks at a hotel." Evie wiped her eyes.

"But where to?" Evie wondered, putting down the knife, screaming.

"I knew this was too good to be true!" Evie kicked the table.

Everything on it fell. "What day is it?" Evie walked over to the TV and turned to the news. She walked away and picked up the bottle from the floor. Evie listened to the broadcast. A special report appeared on the station.

"Yes David, I am here, live at the terror on Columbia Way on the corner of Ross Boulevard. One hundred people have been murdered at the Rock Stone Strip Club earlier this morning. We have never experienced such a horrible sight." Reporter Jan proceeded while Evie dropped the liquor bottle onto the floor. It shattered. Evie is shocked!

"Ambulances traveled from surrounding, cities to help clear out the facility. We have never experienced a scene like this before. Once the bodies are cleared from the club, investigators will do a thorough search. Will all parents who knew of a loved one attending this club or working as an exotic-dancer please come to Savannah Medical Center to help identify bodies?" Evie walked over to the phone and called the front desk again.

"Hello this is Evie Young from room 666. Can someone just charge my credit card from the information I gave when I checked in? I can't find my card at the moment, and I don't feel well." Evie spoke in despair. The attendant agreed.

"Thank you." Evie replied.

"Miss Young do you need us to call 9-1-1?"

"No, I just need to rest." Evie stated.

"That's fine ma'am, you have until noon tomorrow to check out.

"Thank you." Evie hung up the phone and walked slowly toward the TV to turn it off. Instantly, Evie ran into the bathroom and regurgitated and then kicked the door close.

◆◆◆◆◆

The Spirit of the God spoke to Bishop Klein. **"Son it's time, wake-up."** Bishop Klein awaked. Sitting up in bed he slid his legs out from underneath the covers, his feet hit the carpet floor. He glanced at his wife while she remained asleep. He walked toward the bedroom door heading downstairs, not noticing the black suit hanging on the door.

"Son, rest in me, for I will comfort you. Today is a day of many tears. I Am your Father and I will heal your broken heart, but today is a day for rest. Turn on your TV and watch the news." The Spirit of God instructed him. Bishop Klein walked over to the television and turned it to the news. He reviewed the repeated news. Suddenly his spirit became unrested.

"Go wake your wife and you both go to Savannah Medical Center." The Spirit of God instructed. Mr. Klein wept profusely. Leaving the TV on, he walked back upstairs. Making it to the top, he stared at the black suit that hung on their bedroom door. Slowly he walked over to his wife in bed, in tears of mourning. Rising up, Deborah sat uprightly in bed looking at her husband.

"The time has come to say good-bye Kenneth to the last bearing of my womb." She stared at him in sadness. Kenneth sat on the side of the bed weeping in his wife's arms. Deborah touched his head. "We must go to Savannah Medical Center." He spoke and sat up.

"On the news this morning one hundred people were murdered last night at one of the strip clubs." Deborah remained

unresponsive to the news. In a daze, a vision of Sheila flashed before her.

"Honey." Deborah stood, walking toward the black outfit, and touched it. A vision flashed of her ministering at her daughter's final farewell. "Come on. Let's obey and go to the hospital." Kenneth agreed with his wife by nodding.

◆◆◆◆◆

Evie walked out of the bathroom meeting a tall angel in her room. *"You must leave this town NOW... Take the bus to Atlanta, Georgia. Call for the next available bus and get on it. You must obey."* The angel spoke and disappeared. Evie fell on her knees and cried.

"God, please help me! I can't take this any longer. Why me? Why! Evie sighed.

"This is a never-ending nightmare. But... I thank you for getting me out of the club. God, I need to hear your voice. Please help me?" Evie spoke in frustration. An angel of light stood over her. "Just listen and obey!" Evie heard strongly and felt a presence in the room. She jumped and turned around to no one.

◆◆◆◆◆

The Klein's arrived at the Medical Center. They jumped out the car, walking quickly through the front doors and toward the emergency desk. "Yes, we would like to inquire about the one hundred bodies murdered earlier this morning." The bishop inquired at the front desk.

"What's her name?" The clerk questioned.

"Sheila Monica Klein." Deborah answered the nurse rather anxiously. The nurse picked up the phone, dialing another

extension. "Yes, Sheila Monica Klein." The nurse paused to listen on the other end.

"Okay, thank you!" She hung up, and then directed her eyes towards the Kleins. She pointed straight ahead.

"Mr. and Mrs. Klein, if you take this elevator to floor B, it will take you downstairs to the morgue. Doctor Rena will further assist you."

"Thank you!" The Klein's swiftly headed to the elevator. Deborah stood patiently. The doors opened. A man held his wife up in the elevator while they exited. Bishop and Mrs. Klein looked at each other and walked in. They pressed B. The doors closed.

Mrs. Klein squeezed her husband's hand. "The Lord is in charge Kenneth!" Deborah reinsured him. Kenneth looked at her, closed his eyes and shook his head. The elevator doors opened to a lobby with white wallpapered walls and wooden cushioned chairs. They stepped off the elevator. A female doctor in a white smock and clipboard greeted them.

"Mr. and Mrs. Klein?" The doctor questioned.

"Yes. We are here to identify our daughter, Sheila Monica Klein." The doctor checked for that name. "I'm Doctor Rena. Please follow me." Mr. and Mrs. Klein followed her down a dim lit hallway. The bishop held Deborah's hand. Tears formed in his eyes. They stopped and looked at the name, labeled on the refrigerator.

"My God." Bishop mourned in great distress as they walked inside the cold room.

"Is this your daughter?" Doctor Rena walked in and uncovered the body.

"Oh God!" Bishop cried out. Deborah held him up.

"Lord, we need your strength." Deborah asked inwardly. She closed her eyes tightly as tears ran down her face. She looked at her only daughter. A cold wind passed through her, taking away her strength.

"My only baby is gone forever! I never thought I would live to see you descend into eternal hell. You chose to live your life on earth that way." Deborah thought to herself while remaining strong for her husband. Kenneth laid his head on his daughter's stomach as tears dripped onto her cold body.

"Why Sheila? Why didn't you listen to the Spirit of God, who constantly spoke to you? We loved you! You chose the devil's plan and here we are. He is a thief, that comes to steal, kill, and destroy. John 10:10, you knew that scripture all too well." The bishop held his head up, looking at Shelia's still face. Mrs. Klein began to call on the name of Jesus for strength and wept.

"I'll be outside the door." Doctor Rena gently spoke.

"No!" Bishop stopped her from walking away.

"You can cover her back up!" Bishop Klein pulled himself together. They held hands and walked out of the room. Doctor Rena covered Sheila's body and exited.

"Deborah, I'm going to take a walk down the hall." Kenneth spotted the news on the lobby television. Mrs. Klein talked with

Doctor Rena, while glancing at her husband. Bishop looked up attentively at the latest news.

"Hi, this is Jan, once again reporting live about the terror this morning at Rock Stone Strip Club. Officers have arrested 22-year-old Tank Madison and 30-year-old Tracey Mix. The two gentlemen were owners of Rock Stone Strip Club. Apparently, the two gentlemen were not at the club at the time of this incident. Investigators have recovered forty kilos of cocaine from the scene." The reporter announced. The bishop walked closer to the TV observing.

"One hundred pounds of marijuana was found in Tracey Mix's Bentley, concealed inside of a suitcase located in his trunk. In addition, Officer Bradley researched the gentlemen's profile, finding out the following: they were affiliated with the Italian Mafia. Thirty-year old, Tracey Mix was arrested five years ago for picking up a con – A female undercover cop who played the role of a prostitute. He was released 18 months later. That was his first offense."

"The gentlemen pimped women and had sex with them. They spent hundreds to thousands of dollars on these ladies, accounting to the evidence." The reporter stated. "Officer Bradley found a total of $800,000 in receipts spent within a few days. There's a receipt for $60,340, spent on a Mercedes GLS 450, paid in full. Another receipt, for $10,000, that was spent in different upscale fashion and exotic stores. Mr. Mix also purchased a three floor, condominium for $400,000, including $300,000 worth of furniture. And $29,656 was spent on other necessities and restaurant expenses." The bishop closed his eyes and shook his head in disbelief.

"Rock Stone will no longer be in business. We will keep you updated on the latest news. Again, the Savannah Medical Center

still has many unidentified bodies. So please, if a loved one have not returned home last night, or if you were aware of them being an exotic dancer, visit the Savannah Medical Center. Coming to you live from Savannah, Georgia with Channel Two News." Jan reported.

Deborah walked up and stood by her husband. He looked at her sadly. The Kleins took each other's hand and walked toward the exit, until they were interrupted.

"Mr. and Mrs. Klein, we give our condolence for your lost. Whenever you're ready, please contact your local funeral service so they can arrange to pick up the body." The mortician stated.

"Thank you. We will." Mrs. Klein gave the mortician a dry smile. Mr. Klein's cell phone rang. He looked at its caller ID.

"It's Junior." The bishop told his wife. They both looked at each other.

"Hello son, we were just about to call you."

"Something is wrong, isn't it?" Kenneth Jr. replied.

"I heard about the hundreds of people getting murdered in Savannah. The Spirit of God placed upon my heart to call you and mom. Did you get a chance to talk to Sheila?" Their son inquired. Bishop Klein stopped and dropped his head. He cried silently.

"Dad... talk to me! Something's wrong, isn't it?" Kenneth, Jr. questioned. "The whole time I was teaching my last class, I kept seeing Sheila flash before me." Their son shared. The bishop picked his head up and proceeded toward the exit door.

"When that happens, God is trying to tell me something. Right Dad?" Bishop held the phone to his son's question.

"Dad?!" Kenneth Jr. began to worry. "Son, your mother and I will be back in Atlanta by this afternoon. We will talk then. Your mother and I would like to thank you for being in charge and handling the Lord's work while we were gone" The bishop sighed and wiped his eyes.

"You're welcome dad!" Kenneth, Jr. replied.

"We love you son. Talk to you soon." Deborah stared at her husband while listening to their son.

"Okay, talk to you soon." The Klein's son hung up.

"He knows, Kenneth." Mrs. Klein addressed her husband. He looked at his wife nodded his head in agreement. He grabbed his wife's hand and they walked to their car. The assignment God had given them in Savannah was now completed.

Chapter Twelve
Mercy Told Grace

Evie walked out of the hotel toward the bus stop, spotting a dumpster. Walking toward it, she threw her entire suitcase in it. Evie looked at her bus ticket realizing that the bus was parked directly in front of her. She contemplated whether or not she should've gotten on.

Evie mumbled to herself. "I might as well be dead! It really doesn't make a difference anymore. My entire life is pure hell, and it seems like a never-ending cycle. Maybe, if I had stayed at the club and allowed Tira and Sonny to kill me, I'd be out of all my misery." The bus driver opened the door. Evie held her ticket in her hand, while the bus driver made an announcement.

"Everyone please take out your tickets."

"This is the express-route going to Atlanta, Georgia. Evie stepped onto the bus. The bus driver took her ticket and smiled at her.

"It can't be all that bad!" The bus drive commented with a smile. She looked at him with a straight face. "If you only knew!" Evie thought to herself, walking to the back of the bus. The window seat, she sat, staring at pedestrians who walked past the bus.

"I hope no one sits next to me. I really don't feel like being bothered with anyone, at this point." Evie's thoughts went wild, placing her head back, she closed her eyes with a sigh. The bus slowly began to pull off. The bus driver made a departing announcement.

◆ ◆ ◆ ◆ ◆

Bishop and Mrs. Klein traveled to Atlanta. They drove in silence. Mrs. Klein rested on the passenger's side with closed eyes, as the Spirit of God ministered scriptures to her. **"Daughter blessed are you who hunger now, For ye shall be filled. Blessed are you who weep now, For you shall laugh."** [Luke 6:21]

Mrs. Klein placed her right-hand on her mouth, cropping her chin. The loss of her daughter began to weigh heavily on her. Teardrops fell from the corner of her left eye, and then poured from the corner of both eyes. Mrs. Klein squeezed them tight until water flooded her face. She sniffed and wiped her nose. Bishop Klein looked over, after he overheard his wife's sniffles. He saw tears that ran down her face. He placed his right-hand on her knee, turning his head and glanced.

"What went wrong?" Deborah questioned her husband. **Beloved, I have given My people choices. Sheila chose death. You know My word. I told you in the last days that, men shall be lovers of their own selves, covetous, boasters, proud, blasphemers, disobedient to parents, unthankful, unholy. Without natural affections, trucebreakers, false accusers, incontinent, fierce, despisers of those that are good, traitor heady, high-minded lovers of pleasures, more than lovers of God** [2 Timothy 3:2-4]. **Sheila loved self-pleasure more then she loved my Me. She became rebellious and resentful of your authority. So, trust that you have done all I have commanded. Now, just rest in Me."** Spoke the Spirit of the God through the bishop. They exited off the freeway approaching a red light.

"Yes Father, we put our trust in you!" Mrs. Klein wiped the tears from her face. Bishop drove into the parking lot of Kings and Queens of Faith University, preparing himself to deliver the news. They got out of the car; bishop looked up to the sky for strength. He closed the driver side door, and then walked to the passenger's side, opening the door for his wife.

"Thank you for your strength, Father!" Bishop spoke into the air. Mrs. Klein stepped her right foot onto the cement, while stepping out of their luxury car. Bishop closed the door behind her. The two held hands and walked toward the entrance of the school. They entered into the University.

"Hello Bishop and Prophetess Klein. It's good to see you both." Corey, the security guard, greeted.

"Thanks son! It's good to be back!" The bishop and Deborah slightly smiled at Corey. They both walked through the security scanner and up the east wing stairwell. Meanwhile, Corey paged Minister Klein, II.

"Minister Klein your parents are on their way up." Corey informed. "Thanks Corey." Minister Klein, II called into his father's office. Bishop Klein walked into the phone ringing.

"Hello," The bishop answered.

"Hey Dad, I'll be right over!" Kenneth Jr. swiftly hung up. Bishop looked at Deborah. "How did he know we were here?" They grinned and stared at each other. "Corey!" In unison they agreed. Deborah watered the flowers in their office as she looked out the window at the blue sky.

"You are like the flowers you are watering." The Spirit of the God spoke to Deborah, she smiled. "Lord, are you trying to tell me something?" Deborah had conversation with the Spirit of God inwardly.

"Yes. I am watering you and as you thirst for Me, you will grow like this plant. The only difference is you'll never wither away as long as you stay in my Presence." Deborah smiled at God's word

spoken to her. Their son entered the office walking slowly as he hugged his parents, hugging his dad firmly. The bishop phone rang.

"Good to see you mom." Deborah kissed her son on the cheek with a motherly hug.

"How are you son?" Deborah questioned as tears fell from her eyes. He looked over his mother's shoulders at the intense look on his father's face. He remembered when his grandmother died. His father had the same tense look. Kenneth, Jr. discerned that something is definitely wrong. The bishop finished up his phone conversation.

"Yes, 3 p.m. tomorrow will be fine. Thank you." Bishop hung up the phone with sadness. "Son I just got off the phone with the Savannah Medical Center," he sighed.

"The dream you had about your sister not turning from her wicked ways has come to pass." Bishop looked over at his wife.

"Sheila was murdered during a shootout in Savannah. I just received information about her autopsy." The bishop displayed sorrow as water filled, he eyes.

"The doctor found cocaine in her blood along with eight bullets to her heart. They also found $50,000 in her purse."

With two hands, Minister Kenneth, II stood up and slapped his father's desk. His face flooded with tears. He left out, and went into the hallway, where he ran until he fell to his knees.

"Why Sheila, why couldn't you listen. You were so talented, and so

153

smart, and so beautiful, and you were my only little sister . . . I hate you Satan!" Kenneth Jr. cried out. "Do you hear me? I hate you!!! You are going to pay for this." Kenneth mourned in deep sorrow. Corey heard a voice crying out in the hallway. He hiked the stairwell military-style, to find Kenneth Jr. on his knees.

"Minister Klein, are you okay man?" Corey slowly walked towards him. "My little sister is dead. She's gone man, eight bullets to the heart!" Kenneth, Jr. shared as tears continued to stream down his face. Corey kneeled down, wrapping his arms around him.

"Sheila was only 20. Just 20 years old, man!"

"Man! I'm so sorry about your sister." Corey comforted Kenneth Jr. "I told her to repent before the Lord and turn from her wicked ways. God would have forgiven her. He's so faithful. But I guess it doesn't matter now!" Kenneth Jr. broke down.

"You can receive salvation all day, but if you backslide and harden your heart and don't come into repentance, demons will enter in and rule your life! Sheila knew the word of God, but she became rebellious." Kenneth Jr. took out a handkerchief from his suit jacket pocket and blew his nose. Corey backed up, giving him space.

"I love you man! And I'm here if you need me." Corey showed sympathy with a smile. "Cast your cares upon the Lord, man. God will keep you." Corey encouraged.

"Thanks, man!" Minister Klein, II replied, wiping his eyes.

"I'll see you later." Corey smiled and walked back to the security desk.

"Thanks again!" Kenneth Jr. walked back into his parents' office.

"Sorry about that." Kenneth, Jr. apologized.

"There's no need son. we understand!" Bishop cracked a dry smile.

"Do you need me to help do anything?" Kenneth Jr inquired.

"Yes, we do. Here's a list of contacts. Call them and let them know what has happened." The bishop handed Kenneth, Jr a folder. Deborah walked behind their son interrupting. "Give me half of the list and I will help you." Deborah smiled at her son.

◆ ◆ ◆ ◆ ◆

Evie viewed the beautiful trees from her window. "I once was pure as the trees. Now, I feel like the New Jersey River, dirty!" Evie thought to herself. "Now, I see why this world is a collection of errors by one man's disobedience. My wrong motives is a curse from my parents." Evie vents within as tear fell down her face. She slouched down in her seat.

"I lived the way I was taught, and I lived the only way I knew how." Evie continued to stare at the trees as the speeding bus passed them.

"I've done the best I know how to do. Now, look at me! I've failed in everything. I am 17, and I don't even have my diploma!" Evie poured her heart out while tears cause her to breathe harshly, clogging her nose. She placed her hand over her face while tears continued to flow. Evie closed her eyes and drifted off into a comfort zone. Remembering her fun days growing up, Evie thought about her long-lost friend Torri and her whereabouts. Torri and Evie grew up as best buddies. Evie loved chocolate chip

155

cookies. Torri gave Evie the last chip from her cookie after Evie had eaten hers. Ada was known for her homemade chocolate chip cookies and fresh squeezed lemonade she made everyday when they came home from school. Evie reminisced about her mom.

"Torri, Evie, your snack is ready! You girls clean your hands and face before coming into the kitchen," Ada instructed them. Evie smiled daydreaming.

"Hey Evie when we grow up let's go into business together. We can have our own chocolate chip cookie factory" Evie thought about her and Torri's plan as kids.

"I can dig that, but what will we name it?" Evie questioned Torri's idea.

"Oh, I got it . . . What about, Cheer-a-Chip?" Evie suggested excitedly, while Torri smiled. "Not bad!" Torri agreed.

"Not bad right! I like it too." Evie smiled in thought.

"There are many things I would like to become. I do know that I want to work for myself." Evie smiled at Torri dreams.

"And I believe that's why we are best friends, because we like the same things." Torri placed her arm around Evie's shoulder. The two girls smiled at each other, and then dipped their cookies into their lemonade. Evie continued to dream in her comfort zone about the time Torri, Justin, and she went with her parents to their grandparents' church. They ate candy to help them stay awake. When her grandpa or grandma would preach, they had the entire congregation sleep. Evie couldn't wait until service was over, so they could go out as a family to their favorite restaurant.

"Attention all passengers, in about 15 minutes, we'll be arriving in downtown Atlanta. This will be our final destination." The bus driver announced. Evie remained in a daze, not hearing the announcement. She scrunched her forehead while her eyes remained shut. Thinking about the time she cuddled in her mother's lap and her dad tickled her feet. Joy filled her heart on those memories.

"I felt like a princess when my father treated mommy and me special." Evie continued to reminisce. "I wish I could've held on to those realities of good times." Evie spoke to herself, opening her eyes.

"My chances of seeing them all again are hopeless!" She stared out the window at the city of Atlanta. "Why am I here?" Evie stated looking up at the tall buildings.

"Why not Arizona where it's hot and desolate? There, I might have a better chance of dying from thirst rather than pain!" Evie thought.

"All passengers, I would like to welcome you to downtown Atlanta, Georgia. Please remain seated until the bus has come to a complete stop. Make sure you take your belongings with you. Anything left in the overhead compartment, Greyhound will not be held responsible for. And thank you for choosing Greyhound! "All of my baggage is inside of me." Evie mumbled to herself!

Chapter Thirteen
On the Run

"When you get off the bus, turn right." The Spirit of God spoke within Evie. When Evie stepped off the bus, she looked around deciding on which way to go.

"Go left, someone is waiting to give you some money." Evie shook her head in confusion. She observed the scenery and the people around her. Evie chose to go left.

"I hope I don't get lost in this big old city." Where Evie thoughts, as she walked down the busy street.

◆ ◆ ◆ ◆ ◆

Mrs. Klein sat in her office reading over paperwork at her desk, until the Spirit of God interrupted. **"Beloved, pray fervently for Evie. Dispatch her protecting angels and assign them to clear her path so no harm won't come near her dwelling. The spirit of confusion is at hand."**

"In the name of Jesus, Lord, I ask that you send Evie's protecting angels forth, clearing her pathway. Make sure no harm comes near her dwelling. Send laborers across her path to guide her. Lord, continue to order Evie's footsteps and allow her not to fall into the trap of Satan, in Jesus' name, Amen!" Mrs. Klein prayed.

◆ ◆ ◆ ◆ ◆

The busy environment surrounded Evie as she walked down the unfamiliar street. A couple of thugs stood on a corner.

"What's up shorty, what's your name?" A strange young kid asked, as he walked behind her. Evie continued to walk, ignoring him.

"Wait up shorty! Oh, it's like that! Forget you then." The young boy replied while sticking up his middle finger. He approached another cutie that walked by. Evie walked past a wino who stood in an alleyway staggering. The homeless laid around everywhere. Some stood with their hand out asking for money, while others displayed signs that said, 'Feed me, I'm hungry.' Evie weep.

"All the riches in this world and nobody can help these people. They give up nothing and yet they look down on the poor and treat them like they're dirt." Evie thought. Her high-heel boots click clock on the ground, Evie dug into her pocket as she walked in the alleyway. A homeless lady with a small infant took the $100 out of her hand.

"Thank you and God Bless." With a smile the homeless lady spoke.

"You're welcome. Get your baby and yourself some food to eat and maybe a room." Evie smiled with compassion, and then walked away.

Unfamiliar voices began to echo Evie's ears. Suddenly, a large angel appeared in front of her, who pushed her behind a wall to hide her. Evie peeked out.

"Tira and Sonny!" Evie whispered to herself, watching them walk up to a door and changed drugs for money. They shook hands with a brown skinned man with dreads.

"What are they doing in Atlanta?!" God, please protect me from those crazy fools! I knew I should've gone the other way when I got off the bus." Evie spoke out loud to herself and sighed. "Man, everywhere I turned there's trouble!" Looking down at her boots, Evie thought to herself. "I need some sneakers and a gun. I'm tired of them two, and somebody needs to finish them! They really

think they are ruling something! And I'm not running anymore!" Firmly Evie spoke and then received a revelation.

"Wait a minute! If they were in Savannah last night at the club and everyone got killed except them, that means they . . ." Evie eyes enlarged from her conclusion. Tira and Sonny walked towards the alleyway. Evie continued to hide behind the wall. The angel shielded her.

"Are we going to Sheila's funeral tomorrow? They've been talking about it all over the radio and news. Apparently, her parents are these known 'spiritual leaders' here in Atlanta." Sonny sarcastically stated to Tira. They passed Evie, walking across the street toward Tira's cherry-colored Escalade. Evie watched them get in, and then exited the alley as she walked fast in the opposite direction. She ran breathing heavy.

"I am so tired of being on the run. If this doesn't end soon, nobody will have to kill me. I'll do it myself." Evie walked looking over her back in frustration.

◆◆◆◆◆

Tira and Sonny ride with their music thumping while cruising down Peachtree Street. "There's your holy-roller cousin Torri, with that white chick. Aren't you going to blow your horn?" Sonny questioned Tira.

"Hell, no! I'm not blowing at her. That's one chick I'm tired of, too. She thinks she's so 'Holier than Thou', believing in some God that keeps her broke." Tira mumbled. "Her and her white snow cone friend. You blow at her!" With attitude Tira told Sonny.

"I will!" Sonny attempted to blow Tira's horn, but she blocked her.

160

"In your own ride!" Tira displayed a mean face.

"Why are you dogging on your cousin like that?" Sonny asked in a serious tone.

"And why are you taking up for her? You want her too, the way you wanted that Evie chick?" Tira looked at Sonny with a straight face.

"I'm happy that ho is dead! Too bad everyone else had to die because of her. Straight gangster move!" Tira laughed at herself while she kept her eyes on the road, speeding up.

"What's up with you? And...slow down! Why are you driving like you're on crack?" Sonny stared at Tira. "Your mother on crack!" Tira lashed back with attitude. A slap to the face, Tira is angry.

"I don't know what type of demon has possessed you. But...the cops wouldn't have to worry about finding you because I'll finish yo ass myself! Don't you ever put my mother in your mouth!" Sonny mumbled furiously! You straight up trippin!"

"Whatever! I'm tired of yawl Atlanta chicks, especially you!" Tira rolled her eyes, turning off Peachtree, unto a side street. Sonny took out a lollipop, unraveled it and licked it in Tira's face.

"Atlanta chicks...hmmm, you don't say that when I'm..." Sonny licked the lollipop provocatively, and then slouched back in her seat smiling. Tira turned up the music, ignoring her.

◆ ◆ ◆ ◆ ◆

Evie walked out of the sneaker store, smiling looking down at her feet. "These feel nice!" Evie spotted a gun shop.

161

"I am ready now, for whatever comes my way." Evie thought as she walked down the street, stopping abruptly looking at her boots in the bag.

"I need to get rid of these. Being on the run, I don't need any baggage trailing along with me." Evie spotted a dumpster across the street, walked over, and tossed it.

"Welcome to Atlanta's Summer Fair at Piedmont Park." Evie read the sign. "Well, it wouldn't hurt to add some excitement to my life." Evie talked to herself.

"Besides, I don't know what tomorrow will hold." Evie thought to herself, watching families who walked in the park. She stared at an Afro-American woman, who laughed with her daughter, holding her hand.

"If my mom was around, I wonder what we would be doing?" Evie continued to observe parents walking with their children, teenage daughters laughing and walking with their moms, while husbands and wives held hands.

"My parents were so wrapped together in love; nothing could split them up. Now where are they? Only God knows, and I wish I knew! But I guess it doesn't matter anymore. I'm grown and I don't need them now!" Bystanders stared at Evie while she talked to herself.

Watching over her shoulder, Evie continued to walk through the fair and all of the sudden, her mode changed to sadness. She stopped to look at the animals.

"Hmmm...I should buy a dog! Such a cutie! At least someone would love me!" Was her thought. Evie continued to look behind

her as she's drawn to a young lady. "Hmmm." Evie turned around and continued to look ahead. The young woman stared at Evie from behind.

"The young lady who just turned around ten feet in front of you is Evie. Walk closer and call her name. She'll answer." The Spirit of God spoke.

Testing the Spirit to see if that was God who spoke, the young lady walked swiftly. Her brown silk hair flowed in the mild breeze. Walking closer, the fair complexion lady stopped. "Evie!!" Evie heard her name and displayed a strange face. "Damn!" Thought of action ran through Evie's mind, looking at the gun under her shirt.

"Call her by her last name." The Spirit of God spoke within the light complexion young lady.

"Evie Young!" Evie is puzzled about the lady who called her by her full name. She turned around.

"Evie?!" The lady stared at her.

"Yeah, and who are you?" In suspension, Evie looked at the lady while gazing into her eyes. The lady's face lit up in joy.

"It's me Evie, Torri!" Evie is in shocked.

"Torri Mansell!?" "Yes, your 'chocolate chip cookie' eating friend Torri from New York." Torri overwhelmingly spoke.

"Wow! How did you get to Atlanta?" Torri's overjoyed ignored

Evie's question. "I'm sorry to stare... you just don't know how I prayed to see you again! How have you been?" Torri asked with concern.

"Well as least your prayers have been answered!" Sarcastically Evie stated. "Where were you when I needed someone to help me?" Loudly Evie thoughts spoke as she sternly stared.

"Why didn't your mom adopt me?! Maybe, if she had, I would probably still be a virgin!" Evie continued to stare in deep memories until Torri waved her hand in Evie's face.

"I have somewhere to be! Nice to see you." Evie sadly spoke and walked off.

"Hold on!" Torri stopped her.

"This is how you treat a long-lost friend?!"

"You said the key words, 'long-lost' Goodbye!" Rudely, Evie cleared their space.

"Evie, wait! How is your family?!" Torri walked behind her.

"I don't know Torri! You tell me!" Evie stopped with an attitude.

"I'm sorry! I just was wondering when the last time you saw your parents!" Calmly Torri stated.

"Let's see, the last time I saw my parents was the last time I saw you! You do the math!" In frustration she stared, as Torri sighed with compassion.

"Ten years right!" Evie stated, rolling her eyes. First John 1:9 flashed in Torri's head. "Evie is everything okay?"

"No!! And what do you care!?" Evie deeply stared in anger, and then turned around and walked away. Torri insisted on trailing behind her. "Why are you so cold-hearted toward me Evie? I am so glad and thankful to see you again, but you're not!" Torri gave Evie a flier.

"I go to Kings and Queens of Faith University on Kings Boulevard. I've been attending for two years now. We are having a contemporary gospel music concert in four weeks featuring two inspirational artists. I know if you came you will enjoy yourself. Trust me it is not your ordinary Christian college. I guarantee you'll love it." Evie stopped, turned around and overlooked Torri's flier.

"Look! Keep your damn flier! I don't want to go to 'no' gospel concert! And I definitely don't want to see you again. So please... let me be. You are a long-lost friend!!" In bitterness, Evie spoke and walked in the opposite direction. Torri stood speechless with water in her eyes.

"Confess your faults one to another and pray one for another, that ye may be healed. The effectual fervent prayer of a righteous man availeth much." The Spirit of God comforted Torri.

"She will come into repentance. Go in peace and pray." The Spirit of God reinsured Torri." Torri sadly walked back towards a group of friends.

◆ ◆ ◆ ◆ ◆

"Thank you." Front desk handed Evie a keycard as she walked down the carpet hallway of the 5-star hotel. Stopping at the door,

she entered, looking behind her, and shut the door. "I'm exhausted." Evie placed her belongings down and flopped on the bed, closing her eyes and a deep breath. She opened them grabbing the remote and turned to the news. She sat up on the bed.

"This is Carol with CNN News. In the studio today, we give you an update on the tragedy that took place Monday morning in Savannah, Georgia. Officers have arrested Tracey Mix, age 30, and Tank Madison, age 22. Both men have been sentenced to 'life in prison' without bail or parole. Investigators are still looking for the killers. If you have any information regarding this case, please call the station. An elderly witness reportedly saw two young ladies leaving the club, and getting inside a cherry-colored Escalade, shortly after the incident. The license plate number is still unknown." Evie turned off the TV, shook her head in disbelief and flopped back on the bed. Fear fell upon her.

"Tira and Sonny! Oh . . . My . . . God! This a nightmare. Evie stated.

"Oh yeah, I can't walk these streets without being strapped. Those chicks are as crazy as my family. But I refuse to be their victim!" Evie claimed rather boldly.

The gun she purchased, Evie took it out, looked at it and kissed it. "If I have to use this baby, oh well I will." Evie placed the gun on the nightstand laid down and closed her eyes to rest.

◆ ◆ ◆ ◆ ◆

Kenneth, Jr. sat home in the brightness of the morning sun while studying the Bible. He prepared for his message to deliver at his sister's viewing later that evening. Sitting at the table, he listened to the Spirit of God who spoke a message into him.

"My son what I would like you to speak about is, Obedience. It's far greater than sacrifice. One reason young people die at an early age is because they fail to surrender to me and my ways. They love and chase after what they see in this evil world, rather than loving and chasing after me." The Spirit of God continued to speak.

"Son, every time your parents told you something, did it not come to pass?" The Spirit of God questioned him.

"Yes, it did." Kenneth answered inwardly.

"That is the reason why obedience is far greater than sacrifice. You can't see obedience. You can only trust it for what it is: faith. Faith is the substance of things hoped for and the evidence of things not seen [Hebrews 11:1]." Kenneth shook his head in agreement with the Spirit of God.

"Spiritual death is spreading through humanity. People would rather sacrifice to receive prestige, honor, and status than to be obedient and possess the land and reign." Kenneth Jr. listened while the Spirit of God continued to minister to him inwardly.

"Adam and Eve were disobedient to My command. I had prepared what I had for them, but I commanded them to not partake of something that I did not prepare for them, and because they disobeyed, they died spiritually. My people are still dying today, even after I sent my son Jesus. They are partaking of things of the world that I have not prepared for them. So, give my people that example of Genesis 2:17. That's why eternal death continued to spread, due to My people wanting to live for themselves instead of Jesus. I prepared Jesus for My

167

people, but they'd rather partake of sin and other idols. My dear son, I sacrificed, Jesus, to save humanity. I have commanded everyone to receive Him in order to have eternal life through me. But still, they refuse to obey my command. Instead, they'd rather sacrifice, then to be obedient." The Spirit of God continued to minister to Kenneth Jr. "Hallelujah!" Kenneth Jr. rejoiced.

"Sheila sacrificed years of going to church, but she never knew Jesus in her heart, only with her mouth. She never lived the life she was taught, nor did she ever repent in her heart. Sheila stayed in her wicked ways. Sheila did not obey me when I sent laborers her way commanding her to turn from her wicked ways. She rejected Me, and because she disobeyed, death was served to the wicked. Many people will come to your sister's viewing that are headed to hell. And this memorial service is a warning for all who sit amongst you in the room. If they refuse to listen, you will hear soon of a greater terror over the news." The Spirit of God has Spoken.

Chapter Fourteen
Wake-Up Call

Bishop Klein unlocked the doors to the church and patiently waited for the mortician to deliver Sheila's body. As he walked toward the altar, the florist approached the doors.

"Are you Bishop Klein?" The florist asked, as he turned around.

"Yes." He answered.

"I came to deliver your flowers." A short, Caucasian guy replied.

"Okay, come right in! You can set them up right at the altar," Bishop instructed him. Three other guys came in along with him. They each carried a large stand of flowers. They walked back and forth, until all of the flowers were delivered. Bishop Klein walked to the pulpit toward the back of the choir stand to adjust the room temperature. His wife entered the room, looking at the lovely flowers. She inhaled their fragrance. Bishop turned around and smiled at her.

"Honey, I am going out to pick up my suit for tomorrow. Do you need anything?" Deborah stated with a smile. "Yes baby." The bishop replied with a smile. "I need for my darling wife to hurry back!"

"No, my son." The Spirit of God quickened Bishop's spirit.

"You go, and let your wife stay at the church." The Spirit of God instructed. "Baby... on second thought, I will run the errands you need me to run. You stay here at the church." Bishop insisted

as Deborah smiled. "Okay honey! I love you Bishop Kenneth Klein." Deborah honored his position with joy. "And I love you." He kissed his wife bottom lip. With a smile, he walked down the aisle, and then exit. Deborah rested her eyes on the ceiling as the sunlight beamed on her brown face.

"Excuse me, ma'am..." a voice snapped her out of her peaceful state, Deborah looked back. "Yes?"

"I'm here to deliver Sheila Klein's body." The funeral director stated.

"Yes, I am her mother. You can bring her body down to the front." Deborah looked at her daughter's gray casket from afar. She stepped to the side, moving flowers out of the way. Strong men walked like soldiers, as their feet heavily brace the deep, wine-colored carpet, placing Sheila's casket accordingly.

Deborah reflected on the old times as she arranged the flowers around her daughter's casket. As she held back the tears, Deborah reminisced on the time Sheila had her first birthday and half of her teeth. Sheila smeared cake all over her hair that day and cried because it fell in her eyes. In grief, she continued to arrange the flowers on the stand.

"Remember when you were five? Your brother walked you into class on the first day of Pre-K. Your father and I had just gotten off the plane from a conference." She slightly grinned, as she talked out loud.

"I remember the day I bought your first training bra. You were nine going on ten." A teardrop dripped; Deborah daydreamed. "You said, momma do I have to wear one of these?" Deborah laughed as tears released. "And I said to you, yes honey you do.

This is a training bra, that will help train nice and plumped fruit."
Deborah cracked herself up in laughter and tears. "These are
fruit?" Shelia pointed to her chest in the dream, as Deborah
laughed.

"Yes, those are your fruit. One day you will use them to nourish
some grandchildren for your father and me." Deborah visualized
the scene like it was yesterday. While placing the flower-stand
towards the head of the casket, Deborah wiped the running tears.

"What happened to the commitment you made with God when
you were twelve? You promised God you'd do His will and not
your own." She walked to the next flower stand.

"You confessed Jesus as your Lord and Savior. Months later, you
were baptized. I explained to you that when you go down in the
water, you are telling God that you are coming up as a new
creature."

Full of grief, Deborah broke down in tears while placing the other
flower stand at the foot of Sheila's casket. In despair, she sat in the
pew, observing the flowers around the casket.

"Shelia, each of the flower stands represents something. The first
one represents God's mercy upon you, up to the very moment the
death angel came for your soul. The black and white floral
arrangement represents the choices you chose instead of God's
plan. And... the pink and yellow arrangement remind me when
you were pure, innocent and our sunshine." The tears flowed.
"God help me!" Deborah placed both hands on her face and cried
profusely.

"2 Corinthians 6:14 it says, "be not unequally yoked together with
non-believers." You got upset when I told you not to bring that

Tira girl into my home. She had many demonic spirits on her. You cussed me out. And, yes, I took it to the Lord in prayer." Deborah continued to pour out. "At sixteen, you started dating, and I gave you the same scripture. I also told you to wait on the Lord and in His right time and season He would bring you a man of God. But you slept with that boy anyway. You got pregnant and he beat you almost to death. Your father almost went to jail that night!" Deborah looked up towards the ceiling.

"You lost the baby! God instructed us to fast for forty days, praying for you, and then turn it over to Him. People from church ministered to you, they prophesied to you, they spoke blessings over your life, and they warned you about the curse of disobedience. So here we are today grieving all because you chose to harden your heart against the Hands that created you." Deborah squeezed her eyelids as the tears continued to fall. In the meanwhile, a vehicle pulled up in the parking lot.

"Your Father pleaded with you, a month ago, before this day. He even offered for you to come home. But you wanted the streets to be your god. You broke the covenant you made with God and committed adultery with the world. You refused to listen to His voice. He gave you warning after warning, and you rejected Him. If only you listened." Tira and Sonny approached the front door of the church.

"Beloved, turn around." The Spirit of God alarmed Deborah.

"Yes, may I help you ladies?" Deborah stood up and walked to the center of the aisle.

"Hello! What time is the viewing?" Tira questioned while Mrs. Klein began to discern. "The doors open at 6 p.m." Deborah replied as the Spirit of God flashed 2 Corinthians 6:14 before her eyes.

172

"I give my sympathy to you and Mrs. Klein. Sheila was a nice girl. May she rest in peace." Deborah saw right through Tira's fake remarks. Sonny zoomed her eyes around the church.

"It's a shame she had to leave here in such a terrible way." Tira replied adding guilt to her comment. Mrs. Klein looked at both ladies and remained silent.

"Well thank you ladies. Now if you will excuse me, I'll see you ladies out. I need to finish preparing." Mrs. Klein walked behind Tira and Sonny. Tira stopped.

"Wait!" Mrs. Klein stared at Tira with a serious face.

"Do you remember me?" Tira waited for Deborah's answer.

"I do!" Mrs. Klein was short with her answer and walked them to the front door.

"See you later. Mrs. Klein." Tira smiled with a giggle. They both exited as Deborah stared at them strangely.

After closing and locking the church doors, Deborah walked to the altar. Her gift of tongues, flowed out of her mouth. As she spoke, the Spirit of God began to show her an open vision of a strip club with dim lights. Suddenly in the vision the lights went out and gunshots fired. Deborah jumped to the excessive screaming she felt and heard while in a daze.

"Go and open Sheila's casket." The Spirit of God instructed. Deborah moved the stand with the black and white flowers and opened the casket. Sheila laid stiff, wearing the black suit Deborah placed on the closet door.

173

2 Corinthians 6:14 flashed before Deborah again, as she stared at her daughter's dead body. Deborah replayed in her mind the conversation she had with Sheila, of not bringing Tira into her house. Mrs. Klein placed her hand over her mouth to keep her lip from shivering. She grieved greatly from the vision the Spirit of God revealed. Deborah turned around looking at the church doors, and then back around to her daughter's body.

"Tira killed Sheila. Tira is at her last chance, and I will give Satan permission to destroy her in sufferings, if she doesn't turn from her wicked ways. Don't allow anger to enter into your heart, Deborah." The Spirit of God revealed.

"The audacity they had to come in here." Deborah spoke in anger and walking towards her cell phone.

"You will not call the cops or turn Tira in. You are to hearken to My voice and when I tell you to move, you move. I will use you to warn her before self-destruction comes her way. Anoint the church and rest in Me, Beloved." The Spirit of God spoke.

With authority, Deborah grabbed the bottle of anointing oil from the side of the podium. Stepping down and marching to the back of the church, she unlocked the doors and opened them wide. Outside of the church, down the brick stairs she goes.

Anointing oil is tossed all around the building and over the brick stairs. In front of the entrance, she diced the oil. Deborah forcefully walked back up the stairs and into the church, throwing oil rapidly all over the seats and carpet. Tears flowed out of her eyes until she reached the front of the altar. "I command you Satan to stay out of here, in the name of Jesus! The blood of Jesus is saturated all over this place. I command you to stay under my feet, in Jesus' name." From the top of her lungs, Deborah shouted.

"If you only had listened Sheila!" Bishop walked in looking around slowly at all of the anointing oil everywhere. He walked behind his wife touching her back gently. Lifting her sorrowful head, Deborah looked at her husband in deep distress. The bishop began to mourn, looking at his wife.

"I know who did it, Kenneth! Satan used her to kill our baby. He's been plotting since the very first day. "Who honey?" Her husband questioned in concern.

"Tira stepped foot in our house. I warned Sheila. I warned her." Mrs. Klein fell in her husband's arms and cried. He embraced her.

"I saw this day, Kenneth...I saw this day! Four years ago, I just didn't know how it would happen. Why Kenneth? Why did our daughter harden her heart against God? Our only Protector! Why?!" Deborah continued to grieve as Kenneth held her tightly. They grieve together, in front of the black and white flowers.

◆◆◆◆◆

Tira walked into the front door of her five-bedroom house, placing her keys on the side table by her couch. In the other hand, she looked over the mail. Shoes flew off her feet, Tira flopped on the sofa to read through her mail. Torri walked downstairs.

"Hey Tira," Torri walked to the front door and opened it. Tira ignored her, so Torri walked in front of her.

"Hi Tira!" Tira looked up from her mail, ignoring Torri, and then rolled her eyes. Torri stared at her, giving her a puzzled look.

"Humble yourself and exit, Torri." The Spirit of God spoke." Torri walked away, and then exited.

"I can't stand that heifer!" Tira looked at the closed door and turned back around to her mail.

Torri walked to her red sports coupe. Unlocking it, she got in. "Lord, I don't know how much longer I can stay here with that girl. You said to stay away from evil, so why did you place me in the house with the devil himself?" Torri questioned God.

"I have placed you there for a season to intercede, minister, and give warning to the wicked. You continue to hearken to My voice, and I will protect you, Torri. I will never leave you or forsake you. Just listen to me and I will never fail you." The Spirit of God spoke Torri nods. "Yes, Father!" Torri drove off.

◆◆◆◆◆

Evie walked out of the hotel looking both ways before she proceeds, making sure her pathway was clear. As usual, downtown is very busy with the flow of traffic and pedestrians. Evie walked, staring at abandoned buildings surrounding her. She crossed over Peachtree Street onto Baker. Two gentlemen stared at her. A strange guy wearing a black and white bandanna approached Evie.

"Yo' mommy, what's your name?" The thug questioned.

"Why?" Evie replied.

"I'm John. Why you uptight?! Want some smoke? That'll get you loose. The young thug slang talked.

"No thank you!" Evie walked off. John looked at her butt switch from left to right. "Wait up! Can a brother get some numbers?" Evie looked at him stiffly and scratched her head.

"I don't think you understand!" Boldly Evie stated. "It's only God who is keeping me from killing someone, including myself. I have had a long life, and I am tired. So please, get the hell out of my face! I don't want trouble." John backed away from Evie, looked her up and down, and then walked off.

"I am hungry." Evie turned the corner and spotted a New York Philly Cheesesteak Restaurant.

"Oh yeah, I could go for a Chicken Philly Cheese." Walking towards it, Evie hesitated.

"No, go to the pizzeria two blocks down. Get a Philly from there." The Spirit of God instructed.

"Aren't you tired of walking? Just go to the New York Philly Restaurant. The pizzeria is too far!" Evie listened to her free-will as she J-walked across the street. Cars blew their horn, she walked quickly into the restaurant. Three people stood in line ahead of Evie, she got online.

"I might as well get my drink while I'm waiting." Evie told herself, walking over to the soda cooler, choosing her desired drink, and then walked back in line.

"Next person in line please." The cashier called the person in front of Evie. Evie looked around the restaurant sensing that something doesn't feel right. The individual placed her order, paid, and then looked back at Evie. Both lady's eyes locked, it's Sonny! Standing in shock, Evie dropped her soda on the floor and jetted out. Sonny looked through the glass window at Evie running down the street. She

turned back around, smiled, and stood to the side, waiting for her

177

food. "Tira will love to hear this!" Sonny laughed to herself. "Thank you." The cashier smiled as she gave Sonny her bag. She grabbed it and exited. Evie ran into an alley and hid inside a dumpster. "God! This is nasty! Damn it!? When will this nightmare stop?" Evie questioned kicking the dumpster from inside. It's echoed.

◆ ◆ ◆ ◆ ◆

Sonny arrived at Tira's house, parking her truck in the garage, and walking through the door, into the kitchen.

"Tira." Sonny called her name, placing their food on the counter. Tira walked down the stairs, in her stylish leather orange fitted jumpsuit. Sonny placed the bag on the counter. Tira walked into the kitchen and picked up the bag.

"What's this?" Tira questioned

"I brought you a Philly." Sonny replied, taking hers out the bag while Tira stared at it. Sonny unwrapped her sandwich and bit into it.

"I hope mines looks as good as yours." Tira jealously stated, as she opened her sandwich.

"Hold up! You brought yourself a Chicken Philly, and you got me red meat?!" Tira raised her voice at Sonny. "I thought you liked red meat, Tira!" Sonny replied sarcastically, biting into her sandwich. Tira stared at her with a smart look.

"I've seen enough red meat for a lifetime, and no, I don't want it on bread" Tira angrily snatched Sonny's sandwich out of her hand, just when she was about to take another bite. Tira slid the sandwich with red meat in front of Sonny.

178

"Here, you eat it." Tira yelled, slowly looking at her.

"Who do you think you're talking to like that?" Sonny swiftly stood and slapped Tira.

"Now you eat it!" Sonny threw the red meat sandwich in Tira's face. She laughed with her red handprint on her fair-skinned face from the slap. Tira looked at Sonny with a smile.

"I didn't think you had it in you!" Tira stated.

"Don't try thing you never had before. It just might kill you!" Sonny bit into her Chicken Philly. "What are you all dressed for anyway?" Sonny questioned, chewing.

"Everyone else is going to Sheila's viewing. Why can't I? After all she was my pimp and ex before you." Tira stated with a chuckle, walking over to the mirror in the livingroom.

"The girl gotta step in style!" Tira admired herself in the mirror. "You are sick! I don't even know why I get down with you like that. You are crazy as hell!" Sonny rolled her eyes in disgrace, as she finished up her sandwich.

"You know you can't resist this Puerto Rican flavor." Tira conceitedly responded. "Whatever!" Sonny replied while taking her garbage to the trashcan. Tira ate her sandwich at the high counter.

"Oh yeah... by the way I saw your girl today!" Nonchalant Sonny stated. "Who?" Tira questioned biting into her sandwich.

"Ocean! You know... that Evie chick!" With humor Sonny announced. Tira spitted her food out into the foil, threw it in the foil, and then aimed it towards Sonny. It bounced off her chest and unto the floor. Sonny looked at the balled-up foil.

"What! And you didn't do anything?" In rage, Tira yelled.

"Why didn't you call me? Ooh...." Tira rolled her eyes in heated! Sonny snatched Tira by her straight, black hair and slammed her face on the counter. Blood gushed out of her nose.

"I told you not to try something you've never had before because it may just kill you, didn't I?" Sonny threatened in heat. "Didn't I?" Sonny slammed her face on the counter, again.

"Didn't I? Answer me!" Sonny slammed her face on the counter harder. Blood splattered on the counter, from her nose, unto Tira's lip.

"Yeah!" Blood covered Tira's face. She stomped up the stairs, speaking in Spanish! Sonny looked at the blood on the counter.

"Don't get it twisted! I may be quiet, but don't..." Sonny fixed her lip to say the "F," cuss word, but she held her tongue. "I am not these A-T-L chicks. I will go straight Jersey-style on your ass. I don't need a gun, just my hands." Sonny grabbed her keys, and left Tira with her own mess to clean up.

Chapter Fifteen
The Power

Torri arrived at the church with Ruth, her best friend. The ushers greeted them at the door. Bishop, Mrs. Klein, and Minister Klein, II, along with other relatives, sat on the first row in front of Sheila's body. Torri quickly glanced at the casket, and then greeted the rest of the family.

"I am so sorry this happened to your daughter." Torri hugged Mrs. Klein with sympathy.

"Thank you, Torri. I know God is in control." Mrs. Klein stated, looking Torri almond shaped eyes. People from everywhere attended the funeral, even those that Sheila's parents never knew. Bishop looked at his watch.

"Who are all these people?" The bishop whispered to his Kenneth Jr. "People who need Jesus." Minister Klein, II told his dad.

"Son, it is 8:00 o'clock. We need to start walking up to the pulpit." Kenneth Jr. nodded his head, agreeing with his father. He stood, and Bishop took his wife's hand. They walked to the pulpit and sat downside, side by side. Officers stood on both sides of the church. Another one remained on the side near the pulpit. Deborah looked at the hundreds of people Sheila had influenced.

"How did Sheila become so popular?" Out of curiosity, Deborah emphasized. Minister Klein, II stood up in front of the podium in preparation of giving a message that God had for him to speak. Tira and Sonny walked through the doors. Deborah spotted them, tapping the bishop. "There she is Kenneth, the one in red." Tira and Sonny sat in the back of the church, on the last row.

"Good evening, everyone. First, I would like to give honor to God, my dad, Bishop Kenneth Klein, Senior, and my mom, Prophetess Deborah Klein, and to my relatives who are visiting from out of town. I thank you all for coming out. It is sad that we have to come together this way. Especially, when it is questionable where a person may have gone after leaving this life. We know that life on earth is not our home and when people pass on, the bible teaches us to rejoice, because to be absent from the body, is to be Present with the Lord. However, that is not always the case. So tonight, we are going to talk about that. I really would like to get deep into what the Spirit of the Lord has to say on tonight. Can you please bow your heads in prayer with me, Heavenly Father . . ." Tira stared at Kenneth Jr. from afar.

"He is kinda cute," With lustful eyes, Tira continued to look.

"But I am not sitting here listening to this fake sh #t. I am an atheist, and I don't know why I came here in the first place. We are our own gods." Sonny looked at Tira and turned her head to her futile gesture. Tira scooted herself over so she could get a better view of Sheila, and then she looked around the church.

"What a good turnout. Don't I feel popular! But I am out...I've seen enough. You comin?" Sonny gave Tira an ugly look upon her question.

"Bye!" Sonny insisted that she left. Tira stood up in the middle of prayer, as the usher tried to stop her until prayer was completed. Pushing through, Tira walked out.

"Look up." The Spirit of God quickened Deborah to open her eyes and observe Tira's behavior. One of the officers watched Tira closely while she exits.

"If all are in agreement, let the church say amen." The congregation agreed. The officer spoke into his radio receiver softly while keeping his eyes stayed on Tira. Sonny remained at the viewing convicted in her spirit concerning the death of Sheila. God began to deal with Sonny inwardly, as Kenneth Jr. ministered.

◆◆◆◆◆

Tira ran down a side street to her SUV, looking behind her. Chirping the alarm, quickly she hopped in. The music blasted as she started the vehicle. In the meantime, Evie woke up, and peeked out of the dumpster door. The coast is clear, she jumped out and gazed in the sky as the sun set.

"Uh . . . my head." A headache caused Evie to place her hand on her forehead as she walked through the alleyway. Proceeding towards her hotel, she looked over her shoulder at an intersection. She looked down a dark street. "Oh... I'm not about to repeat the same thing I went through today by going downside streets. Let me keep my behind on the main streets." Evie convinced herself.

Dark streets with bright lights, Evie crossed over the intersection cautiously as a vehicle spotted a red light. Tira slammed on brakes as she waited for the light to change. Evie noticed the cherry-colored Escalade stopped in front of her, she looked. The two ladies made eye contact. Evie ran, Tira mashed the gas and skidded off. Missing Evie by an inch, Tira turned the corner sharp. Tira leaned over and opened her glove compartment, reaching for her gun. Over the sidewalk Tira drove, not paying attention.

"Damn it Sonny, I need my gun!" Tira drove like a mad woman, hitting the steering wheel. "You know what, I don't need a gun!" Tira pressed down on the gas pedal. Evie dodged Tira, thinking about her contradicting words.

183

"I'm tired of running! You're coming for me Tira, here I am." Evie stopped next to a brick wall.

"God, I'm tired!" In anger she screamed as Tira stopped the vehicle. Evie walked towards her, while Tira hopped out and charged towards her. Before Tira got close enough to Evie, she jumped up and kicked the hell out of her. Down she went. Tira tried to get up until Evie stood over her, kicking her back down and pressed her foot in her chest.

"Why are you after me?!" Evie pressed her foot harder into her chest with rage.

"I don't even know you!" Therefore, I haven't done anything to you! So why are you chasing and threatening to kill me?" Blood dripped down Tira's face, trying to lift her scraped body.

"This is your first and last warning. If you ever come near me again or even think about chasing me down, I'll finish you! If you knew the type of life I've had, you wouldn't f#!k with me! Do you understand me?!" Evie threatened her, releasing her foot off her chest. Tira lifted her head. Evie stepped back in position to take action if she tried her again. "Let's see, if I walk away, will you try to kill me the same way you killed those hundreds of people at the strip club, including Sheila?" "Or should I just go ahead and call the cops and turn you in?" Tira rolled her eyes at Evie as she stepped back into her truck. "I don't know what you're talking about!" Tira drove off quickly.

"I'm so exhausted!" Evie collapsed to her knees in disarray and desperation, she cried out. "God please help me!"

◆◆◆◆◆

"God is calling everyone to obedience." Kenneth Jr. preached.

"There are many here tonight who are living on the edge. If that's you, come to this altar now. Your life is not promised to you. Evil spirits are plotting many of your deaths, and if you think Satan and his demonic spirits aren't real, you are foolish! Look around. Right here in from you, on the news and at every hand." Kenneth looked down and turned the pages.

Kenneth Jr. read, "The thief cometh not, but for to steal and to kill and destroy, I come that they might have life and that they might have it more abundantly, John 10:10." Kenneth Jr. read as the congregation stared attentively in conviction.

"Satan uses many things to entice us away from God. Money happens to be one of the biggest baits of all. Just think about it. Everyone needs money and can't survive without it. And please understand, it's not the money that is evil. It's the love of money over God, that makes it evil. And God knows this! So does Satan! That's why Satan uses material things to lure in souls. He's a thief, a killer and he come to destroy lives, like he did Sheila, my sister." Kenneth Jr. walked towards the edge of the pulpit staring out into the audience.

"There are many people here tonight confused about who they are. If that's you, God is calling you. He loves you, as He loved my sister. But my sister's body is lying here right now lifeless because she chose to live her life how she wanted. God had a plan for her, but she rejected it and harden her heart against Him. Sheila was warned repeatedly to turn from her wicked ways, but she refused to. I guess she thought, choosing her own free will would be better than God's will for her. But here's the thing, Romans 7:18 teaches, And I know that nothing good lives in me, that is, in my sinful nature. I want to do what is right, but I can't. So, if your nature is sinful, yet you choose to live your life on the account of your own free will, your life is full of sin.

185

And the wages of sin leads to death, according to Romans 6:23."
Some of the people in the congregation are convicted by Kenneth
Jr, teaching. They dropped their heads in shame.

"I plead with you right here, right now, to surrender tonight to
God's will for your life through Christ. This could be you next,
lying in a casket and not knowing where your soul will spend
eternity." Kenneth Jr walked down the stairs and stood in front of
the people.

"Ministerial staff, can you please take your position?" Kenneth Jr.
instructed. The ministers dressed in black with clergy collars,
stood in front of Sheila's body. Sonny held her head down,
shaking her head in full surrender as her eyes filled with tears.

"Young people, adults, and everyone who is sitting here right now,
it's no coincidence that you're here tonight. You are God's future
generation. Kenneth Jr. expressed with authority. Sonny looked
up with her face flooded by tears. Kenneth Jr, began to cry, as the
musician played softly.

"I am not going to stand up here and front and pretend as though
hell isn't real! When I was in the world, I walked in complete
rebellion against God. However, I had no peace in my mind or my
life! Every day, I had to watch my back." Kenneth Jr wiped his
tears.

"These are my parents sitting up here." Bishop and Deborah
slightly smiled at their son's acknowledgement. "They poured
nothing but love and the Word of God into my life and into my
sister's. Overtime, I came to true repentance and surrendered to
God. Sheila didn't." Kenneth Jr. sighed deeply.

"I knew this world was full of hell, but I wanted to taste and see

for myself. Now that I am walking faithfully with God, I will never turn back!" Sincerely Kenneth Jr. expressed.

"There are many who are here tonight who have hardened their hearts. They don't want to hear the Word of God. They don't want to step foot into a church unless it's a funeral! You only want to hear what your sinful nature desires, until God sets an example in front of you, like Sheila. You must choose." Kenneth Jr. extended his right hand towards the congregation.

"I am leaving you with this invitation, come to Jesus now! He is your ticket in. Jesus said, I am the way, the truth and the life. No one comes to the Father except through Me, John 14:6." Kenneth Jr, walked towards the middle of the aisle.

"Once you have established a personal relationship with The Living God, you will then have access directly to God. But you must accept his son first. Being in the body of Christ, is your unseen protection. After you have received Him, you can then possess the Holy Spirit, who will guide and lead you into all truth. Sheila rejected the Holy Spirit. That is blasphemy! Therefore, unholy spirits ruled, reign and destroy her life." Kenneth Jr. stopped in the middle of the aisle as he looked around.

"Everyone you see lying in a casket doesn't enter into eternal rest. If you lived a life that is full of hell, wickedness and a harden heart, Matthew 25:41 says, Then shall He say also unto them on the left hand, depart from me, ye cursed, into everlasting fire prepared for the devil and his demons. Living in torment and trauma for eternity was never God's plan for you. But rest assured, you will live in eternal fire, if you don't choose which God you will serve. The God of All Creation, or the god of this life?" Kenneth Jr. emphasized with his hand extended.

"God wants to talk to you and order your footsteps. You'll never

know what's after you until it finds you. And I guarantee, if it's not Christ directing your path, whatever comes your way is destined to capture and destroy you. Facts! Look in the casket." People in the congregation wept under the sound of Kenneth Jr's. voice.

"God doesn't care if you are an alcoholic, prostitute, drug dealer, homosexual, murderer, or fornicator. He loves you! But....He hates the act of sin. Come to Him so He can save you, clean your life up and protect you. I am here to tell you. You'll never get it right alone! You need a Greater Power, stronger than your own free will. So again, everyone who has not accepted Christ into their life, or if you've backslid, come forward now." Worship leaders began to sing as the pianist plays softly. Kenneth Jr. walked towards his sister's casket, viewed her body, and then turned around towards the souls at the altar.

"Come now!" Deborah sang a melody. Souls from all angles of the church made their way up to the altar.

"God is calling you. If you step out this door without receiving Christ, Satan will set you up to destroy your life right before your very eyes. You can be here today and gone tomorrow. God speaks to us, and Satan does too. If you have never received Jesus, and you are hearing a voice telling you, 'Man, you don't need that, you can be your own 'god,' you're being deceived. Don't listen. He's lying to you. The proof is lying in this casket behind me!" Kenneth Jr. pointed as lost souls surround themselves around the casket. Bishop Klein looked at his wife as she sang while many people made their way up to the altar. The ministers, ministered salvation, and deliverance to the people at the altar. Sonny came forth, drenched in tears. One of the altar workers embraced her with love; they began to minister to her.

"That message was just for me! I am tired of being Satan's advocate! Will Jesus accept me, even though I am gay?" Sonny

questioned. "Yes, He will!" The tall fair skinned minister reassured.

"God is no respecter of persons. He can clean up any mess. Allow me to pray the prayer of repentance with you 1John 1:9 and the prayer of salvation, Romans 10:9-10, just repeat after me." Sonny repeated after the minister, as tears drenched down.

Torri and Ruth made their way down the aisle toward the exit. In the meantime, Tira slammed on her breaks in front of the church. Slinged her door opened, she hopped out in anger, and ran into the church. A police officer spotted the cherry escalade, they ran her tags.

Tira stormed into the church with scars and bruises on her face and messed up hair. Torri and Ruth looked over their shoulder as they stood in front of her.

"Tira, what are you doing here? And, what happened to you?" Torri questioned with concern.

"Get out of my way!" Tira pushed her way through Torri and Ruth. She walked toward the altar with an attitude. The officer stood near the altar as he received a call on his radio. The officers' eyes stayed on Tira. "Sonny!" Fiercely she yelled. Deborah sang with her eyes closed, until she's alarmed by the yelling. Widely they opened while the four officers looked sternly at Tira, and she looked at them.

 The minister finished praying with Sonny. Sonny looked up to Tira who stood in her face.

"What the hell are you doing, Sonny?!" With attitude Tira demanded an explanation.

189

"Watch your mouth!" Sonny whispered as Deborah walked down from the choir area towards Tira and Sonny. The police officers walked closer towards Deborah.

"My real name is Sonjeria. Sonny doesn't live here anymore! I just gave my life to Christ, Tira! I'm done living that reckless lifestyle." Sonjeria made her confession. Deborah stood nearby smiling, when she turned around, eight armed officers walked into the church. Four remained at the front door, while the other four walked towards the altar. The souls at the altar where alarmed and began to move out of the officer's way.

Deborah made eye contact with an officer, and then she looked at Tira. Her face lit up.

"I think we should leave now Torri!" Ruth demanded as she proceeded towards exit. Torri gently grabbed Ruth' arm.

"Hold on!" Torri spoke with suspense while the officers began to surround Tira. Anger had blinded Tira from realizing what was going on around her. Sonny looked at the officers behind Tira.

"I have had enough of the street life. I'm done with it, and I am done with you! Homosexuality isn't of God. It's the work of evil, and I am through with it!" Sonjeria glanced at Deborah with a smile. Kenneth Jr looked at his mom, she smiled.

"You're crazy! You're going to walk away from making thousands and thousands of dollars a day to believing in a God who wants you poor and broke. Unbelievable! Tira proclaimed. Deborah stepped in, looking at Tira with sternness. The officers placed their hand on their guns. The officer at the altar walked towards Deborah, positioning himself.

190

"Tira, God is looking at you right now! And He knows exactly what you have done!" Not interested, Tira stared at her .

"And what did I do, 'Preacher's wife!'" Tira sarcastically challenged her. Deborah looked at her calmly as possible, trying to keep from killing Tira herself.

"Repent, Tira! Turn from your wicked ways. Jesus is waiting to save you." Deborah stated. "Go to hell!" Demonically Tira responded. As she began to move, the officers' position their weapons. Tira glanced around and realized what was happening.

"Tira Yukim, you are under arrest! Whatever you say will be used against you in a court of law. You have the right to an attorney," the officers continued to read Tira her rights while hand-cuffing her on the ground. Sonjeria looked at Tira and Deborah as she walked out of the church in tears. Tira silently placed her face against the floor in guilt. The evil spirits began to torment her within. Torri stood astounded, while the officer cleared the premises with Tira cuffed.

Prophetess Klein watched the officers usher Tira out of the church. Bishop walked up to his wife and hugged her as she laid her head on his shoulder. She wept.

◆◆◆◆◆

Sonjeria walked down the street as drops of rain lightly fell. Approaching a corner, she looked up at the streetlights. Rain began to pour down. She freed her long Indian hair out of its ponytail. It hung as she stood in the rain and cried.

"God, I am so sorry for all of the wrong I've ever done! Thank you, for protecting me. What was I thinking? It's only because of Your grace and mercy that I'm not going to jail with Tira. God, teach me your ways. I don't want to live the life I used to. Thank you for

my praying grandmother." Sonjeria stated as she walked across the street and stood underneath a covering from the rain. Dialing numbers on her smart phone, she placed it up to her ear.

"Hello Grandma, this is Sonjeria. I'm tired of being out in the world. I'm ready to come back home. Can I?" Sonjeria asked. She smiled, closing her eyes to her grandmother's voice. "I'm on my way." Sonjeria hung up the phone, placed it in her pocket and ran home in the rain.

◆◆◆◆◆

Evie sat balled up as she transitioned into an alleyway. Rain continued to fall. Through the thunder, a tall angel appeared behind her, a light shined.

"Come and follow Me Evie. I will lead you to rest. God has prepared a place for you. A place you have ran from. But it's time to go back to the help God has sent you. He will unfold the mystery of your family." Evie held her head up. Looking around, she stood up. While walking out of the alleyway, she looked behind and saw nothing but darkness. She continued to walk until she reached a main street. Turning her head left to right she cried out. "Which way do I go? I don't know which way to turn to anymore!"

Evie fell to her knees in tears. She began to bang her head on the concrete ground. Car lights shined on her. Evie looked up. "Tira, if you want to kill me go ahead! I'm too weak to fight anymore!" A car door opened, a woman got out, and stood over Evie.

"It's over, Evie. God said you don't have to run anymore. He's here!" Deborah squatted down and wrapped her arms around Evie. She took off her suit jacket and covered her from the rain. Both ladies walk towards the car, while they held each other tightly.

"Your storm is over now. Let's go home!" Evie stopped in front of the passenger door, and then Deborah stopped. Evie looked at her sternly and cracked a smile.

"You were just in Savannah. What are you doing in Atlanta now?" Evie questioned. "Atlanta is our home. God had me in Savannah on an assignment for several of months for my daughter, and that's when He led me to you. But unfortunately, we are burying our daughter Sheila tomorrow!" Deborah stated as Evie' eyes widen. "Did you say Sheila?" Evie questioned looking in shock.

"Yes!" Deborah confirmed looking at Evie. "No!" Evie stated in disbelief. "Mrs. Klein I am so sorry!" Evie nodded in tears. "Yes, I met Sheila. Deborah discerned with tears that fell from her face. Both ladies hugged tightly.

"God orders the footsteps of the righteous Evie. Even if you don't live a righteous life, God looks at the heart. And it's his grace and mercy that has led you out of harm's way. " Deborah grinned with compassion in her eyes, as she opened the car door for Evie. "Thank you!" Evie stated as the bishop got out of the car and closed the door for Evie and his wife. He got back into the luxury car and drove off.

◆◆◆◆◆

Bishop and Deborah took Evie in as their own flesh and blood. Evie rode in the back seat in peace, as the bishop smiled at her through the rearview mirror. Evie still had many unanswered questions in regard to her parent's. But what she was grateful of that, God heard her cry and gave her a second chance.

Invitation to Salvation

Many of you are probably saying, "Hey this was a great book," and I am so honored that you've enjoyed it. However, the purpose of sharing this prophetic story with you is to highlight some things to you about God. He is a loving and merciful God, and He was loving and merciful to Evie. In spite of what Evie went through, she confessed in her heart and believed that Jesus is Lord. At the very end, Evie fell to her knees and cried out to God, because Romans 10:9 and 10:10 was seeded into her heart. She was tired of the life she was living.

I am here to ask you, are you tired of the life you're living? If so, Jesus is waiting at the door for you with open arms, ready to receive you. He doesn't care how many women you slept with or how many men you been with, or who you slept with last night. If you're a stripper, prostitute, ho, pimp, drug dealer, gay, or have AIDS. Even if you've made some bad choices in your life, God is a God of a second chance. All He care about is you surrendering your life to Him, so that He may give you true life abundantly! He is able to clean you up, heal you, and make it right, as if you were never labeled those classifications of the world. God loves you, that's why He sent Jesus Christ. For, those who believe in Him shall be saved. Revelation 12:11 reads, "And they overcame him by the blood of the Lamb and by the word of their testimony, and they did not love their lives to the death."

Evie's testimony was given so that you can also become an overcomer by the Blood of the Lamb, which is in Christ. At the end of this book, Evie's testimony of surrendering totally to God's will was shared to help you make the same decisions to follow Him. I would like you to pray this first prayer aloud.

First: Come into Repentance
1 John 1:8-9 says, [NKJ], "If we say that we have no sin, we

deceive ourselves, and the truth is not in us. If we confess our sins, He is faithful and just to forgive us of our sins and to cleanse us from all unrighteousness."

"Father, I come before you in the name of Jesus. I repent of all my shortcomings and my sins. I turn away from them and turn to you. I ask you to forgive me for all of the sins I've committed, the sins in my heart and in my thoughts. Thank you, Lord, for your mercy and your grace that endures forever, in Jesus' name, Amen." Once you've come to Jesus and acknowledged you've sinned, He can then save you. Pray this second prayer with me.

Now: Receive Your Salvation

Romans 10:9-10 [NKJV] says: "That if you confess with your mouth that God has raised Him from the dead, you will be saved. For with the heart one believes unto righteousness, and with the mouth confession is made unto salvation."

"Father, I believe that Jesus Christ is the Son of God. I believe He died for me, and I ask you to save me now. Dear Lord Jesus, come into my heart, come into my life, and place my feet on the right path - the path of righteousness and the path of serving you. Thank you, Lord Jesus, in Jesus' Name, Amen."

Congratulations! You have made one of the greatest steps of your life, when praying those prayers. Now, I encourage you to read your bible so you can have a clear understanding of what God expects out of your new life walking with Him. I also pray that God sends laborers out on your behalf, leaders of a good spirit who will disciple and raise you up in the ways of God. I will continuously keep you in my prayers. God Bless!

Meet The Author

Author. Executive Producer & Publisher
Eva M. Bellamy

The director, producer and screenplay writer of the hit stage plays "All My Sisters and Me" & "Holy Seduction," Eva Bellamy knows all too well the consequences for not following her intuition. Eva has traveled a long hard road, following after her dreams, when moving to Atlanta with two small children to open a business, only to find herself homeless 30 days later. When things couldn't get worse for Eva, she lost her job and resorted to becoming a dancer. Over the course of 10 years, Eva found herself sleeping from couches, floors, shelters and in her car, while pursuing her dreams.

Life started to turn for Eva once she began to listen to her intuition and made better choices. That's why her mission is to coach dreamers who are self-driven about entrepreneurship. Eva Bellamy's passion is to help others write their stories and turn their books into screenplays or films. Eva's favorite quote is, "It's the choices you choose, that will make or break you in life."

Product & Services

Sequel: Two

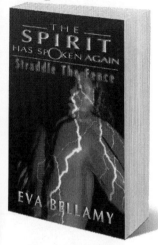

ORDER YOUR COPY!

www.tavpp.com

In the first sequel, Evie Young walked a difficult journey, battling with listening to her intuition. In Sequel Two, "With the mystery that remains, Evie Young still anticipates her parents return with clueless thoughts about their existence. The straight and narrow path, Evie's spirit longs to walk after. But her flesh insists on leading.

Darkness continues to haunt her path. Evie is straddling the fence between good and evil. Brown arms, she deceitfully falls into again. She's attacked through demonic forces, possessed. The ones who were sent to help, Evie rises up against them. Will Evie allow evil to rule her life? Or will she allow the loss of her parent, keep her lost?

197

Now It's Time to Write Your Book!

"Time to Write It," is design to guide you through the process of getting your book, or screenplay written in 30 days. You will have access to me as your writing coach, along with other resources, including a literary agent. Scan the QR code below and let's start today!

MEET YOUR NEW
INSTRUCTOR